STEVE McQUEEN

FULL-THROTTLE COOL

WRITTEN BY
DWIGHT JON ZIMMERMAN
ART BY GREG SCOTT

motorbooks

FIRST PUBLISHED IN 2015 BY MOTORBOOKS, AN IMPRINT OF QUARTO PUBLISHING GROUP USA INC., 400 FIRST AVENUE NORTH, SUITE 400, MINNEAPOLIS, MN 55401 USA

THE INFORMATION IN THIS BOOK IS TRUE AND COMPLETE TO THE BEST OF OUR KNOWLEDGE. ALL RECOMMENDATIONS ARE MADE WITHOUT ANY GUARANTEE ON THE PART OF THE AUTHOR OR PUBLISHER, WHO ALSO DISCLAIMS ANY LIABILITY INCURRED IN CONNECTION WITH THE USE OF THIS DATA OR SPECIFIC DETAILS.

THIS PUBLICATION HAS NOT BEEN PREPARED, APPROVED, OR LICENSED BY THE STEVE McQUEEN ESTATE.

WE RECOGNIZE, FURTHER, THAT SOME WORDS, MODEL NAMES, AND DESIGNATIONS MENTIONED HEREIN ARE THE PROPERTY OF THE TRADEMARK HOLDER. WE USE THEM FOR IDENTIFICATION PURPOSES ONLY. THIS IS NOT AN OFFICIAL PUBLICATION.

MOTORBOOKS TITLES ARE ALSO AVAILABLE AT DISCOUNTS IN BULK QUANTITY FOR INDUSTRIAL OR SALES-PROMOTIONAL USE. FOR DETAILS WRITE TO SPECIAL SALES MANAGER AT QUARTO PUBLISHING GROUP USA INC., 400 FIRST AVENUE NORTH, SUITE 400, MINNEAPOLIS, MN 55401 USA.

TO FIND OUT MORE ABOUT OUR BOOKS, VISIT US ONLINE AT WWW.MOTORBOOKS.COM.

ISBN: 978-0-7603-4745-4

SENIOR EDITOR: DARWIN HOLMSTROM
ART DIRECTOR: JAMES KEGLEY

EDITED BY HOWARD ZIMMERMAN
WRITTEN BY DWIGHT JON ZIMMERMAN
ILLUSTRATED BY GREG SCOTT
COVER AND INTERIOR DESIGNED BY RICHARD AMARI

THIS IS A Z FILE INC. BOOK.

PRINTED IN CHINA

1 3 5 7 9 10 8 6 4 2

CONTENTS

IN 1967, ACTOR STEVE McQUEEN, ALREADY A HOLLYWOOD SUPERSTAR, PRODUCED AND STARRED IN A FILM THAT VAULTED HIM TO THE LEVEL OF A CULTURAL ICON...

BULLITT

THE STORY WAS A COMPLEX TALE OF DECEIT AND ROUGH JUSTICE. IN A PIVOTAL MOMENT, LIEUTENANT FRANK BULLITT, A MAVERICK IN THE SAN FRANCISCO POLICE DEPARTMENT, IS MARKED FOR DEATH BY THE MOB. BULLITT, IN HIS FORD MUSTANG, SEES THE HIT MAN'S DODGE CHARGER AND TURNS THE TABLES. THE HUNTER IS NOW THE HUNTED.

SKREEECH

WHAT HAPPENS NEXT IS A SCENE THAT RIVETED MOVIE AUDIENCES TO THEIR SEATS: A TEN-MINUTE CAR-CHASE THRILL RIDE THROUGH THE STREETS OF SAN FRANCISCO AND BEYOND THAT NOT ONLY DEFINED THE MOVIE...

VVROOOM!!

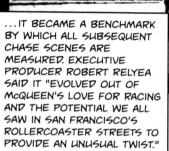

...IT BECAME A BENCHMARK BY WHICH ALL SUBSEQUENT CHASE SCENES ARE MEASURED. EXECUTIVE PRODUCER ROBERT RELYEA SAID IT "EVOLVED OUT OF McQUEEN'S LOVE FOR RACING AND THE POTENTIAL WE ALL SAW IN SAN FRANCISCO'S ROLLERCOASTER STREETS TO PROVIDE AN UNUSUAL TWIST."

ROBERT VAUGHN
SENATOR WALTER CHALMERS

JACQUELINE BISSET
BULLITT'S GIRLFRIEND, CATHY

DON GORDON
SERGEANT DELGETTI, SFPD

SIMON OAKLAND
CAPTAIN SAM BENNETT, SFPD

METICULOUSLY CHOREOGRAPHED AND REHEARSED, SHOOTING STARTED AT 7:30 A.M., LASTED UNTIL DARK, AND TOOK THREE WEEKS. UNLIKE PREVIOUS MOVIES THAT UNDERCRANKED THE CAMERA TO FAKE HIGH-SPEED CHASES, EVERYTHING WAS SHOT "AT SPEED" WITH THE MODIFIED CARS TRAVELING UP TO 110 MPH THROUGH THE CITY'S STREETS.

NORMAN FELL
CAPTAIN BAKER, SFPD

ROBERT DUVALL
TAXI DRIVER WEISSBERG

RELEASED ON OCTOBER 17, 1968, IT WAS A CRITICAL AND BOX-OFFICE SMASH, THE FIFTH HIGHEST GROSSING FILM OF 1968, WINNING AN ACADEMY AWARD (EDITING) AND AN EDGAR AWARD (SCREENPLAY).

K-BWUH WHOOM!

IN 2007, THE LIBRARY OF CONGRESS SELECTED IT FOR PRESERVATION IN ITS NATIONAL FILM REGISTRY FOR BEING "CULTURALLY, HISTORICALLY, OR AESTHETICALLY SIGNIFICANT."

IN AN ACTING CAREER THAT INCLUDED A SUCCESSFUL TV SHOW, *WANTED: DEAD OR ALIVE,* AND ROLES IN SUCH SUCCESSFUL FILMS AS *THE MAGNIFICENT SEVEN, THE GREAT ESCAPE, THE SAND PEBBLES, PAPILLON, THE TOWERING INFERNO,* AND MANY MORE, STEVE McQUEEN WAS THE HIGHEST PAID ACTOR OF HIS DAY AND ACCLAIMED AS "THE KING OF COOL." BUT EQUALLY IMPORTANT TO HIM WAS RACING. IN FACT, IT WAS A PASSION THAT DEFINED HIM.

A LOT OF PEOPLE GO THROUGH LIFE DOING THINGS BADLY. RACING'S IMPORTANT TO MEN WHO DO IT WELL. WHEN YOU'RE RACING, IT...IT'S LIFE. ANYTHING THAT HAPPENS BEFORE OR AFTER...IS JUST WAITING.

ONE

HIS PERSONAL GREAT ESCAPE

TERRENCE STEVEN McQUEEN WAS BORN ON EITHER MARCH 21 OR MARCH 24, 1930, AT THE BEGINNING OF THE GREAT DEPRESSION. HIS FATHER, TERRENCE WILLIAM McQUEEN, WAS A NE'ER-DO-WELL STUNT PILOT WHO ABANDONED STEVE AND HIS MOTHER, JULLIAN, WHEN STEVE WAS SIX MONTHS OLD.

WHEN STEVE WAS THREE, JULLIAN ABANDONED HER SON TO HER PARENTS, VICTOR AND LILLIAN CRAWFORD. WHEN VICTOR'S FARM FELL VICTIM TO THE GREAT DEPRESSION, THEY MOVED IN WITH LILLIAN'S BROTHER, WHOM STEVE CALLED UNCLE CLAUDE.

UNCLE CLAUDE WAS STERN, BUT FAIR. IF STEVE GOT OUT OF LINE, HE WAS PUNISHED. BUT REWARDS INCLUDED, AT AGE FOUR, A RED TRICYCLE.

STEVE BECAME SO GOOD A TRICYCLIST THAT HE CHALLENGED LOCAL BOYS TO RACES--AND ALWAYS WON, CLEANING THEM OUT OF THEIR WAGERED GUMDROPS.

THEN, WHEN STEVE WAS NINE...

UNCLE CLAUDE, I'M TAKING MY SON WITH ME TO CALIFORNIA. WE'RE GOING TO LIVE WITH MY NEW HUSBAND, BERRI.

JULLIAN'S DECISION WAS A TRAGIC MISTAKE. BERRI HATED HIS STEPSON AND REPEATEDLY BEAT HIM.

YOU'RE JUST GETTING WHAT YOU DESERVE, YOU WORTHLESS PUNK!

STEVE BECAME AN ON-AND-OFF-AGAIN MEMBER OF L.A. STREET GANGS.

WHEN POLICE CAUGHT HIM AND OTHER GANG MEMBERS STEALING HUBCAPS, JILLIAN SIGNED A COURT ORDER COMMITTING STEVE TO REFORM SCHOOL.

STEVE SPENT FOURTEEN MONTHS AT THE CALIFORNIA JUNIOR BOYS REPUBLIC AT CHINO. THERE HE MET MR. PANTIER, ONE OF ITS SUPERINTENDENTS.

YES, STEVE, YOU'VE HAD A HARD LIFE. BUT YOU'RE WORTH MORE THAN YOU THINK.

I DON'T KNOW, MR. PANTIER...

I DO, STEVE-- I HAVE FAITH IN YOU.

MR. PANTIER'S PATIENT COUNSELING REACHED THE TEENAGER, AND, REMARKABLY, STEVE SOON BECAME A MODEL STUDENT.

7

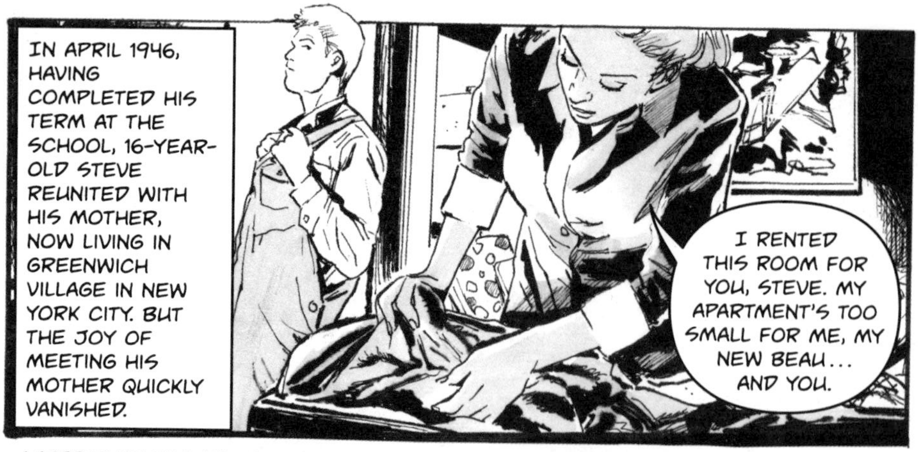
IN APRIL 1946, HAVING COMPLETED HIS TERM AT THE SCHOOL, 16-YEAR-OLD STEVE REUNITED WITH HIS MOTHER, NOW LIVING IN GREENWICH VILLAGE IN NEW YORK CITY. BUT THE JOY OF MEETING HIS MOTHER QUICKLY VANISHED.
I RENTED THIS ROOM FOR YOU, STEVE. MY APARTMENT'S TOO SMALL FOR ME, MY NEW BEAU... AND YOU.

LATER THAT DAY, AN UNHAPPY STEVE CROSSED PATHS WITH TWO MEN FROM THE MERCHANT MARINE WHO TOOK THE BOY TO A NEARBY BAR.

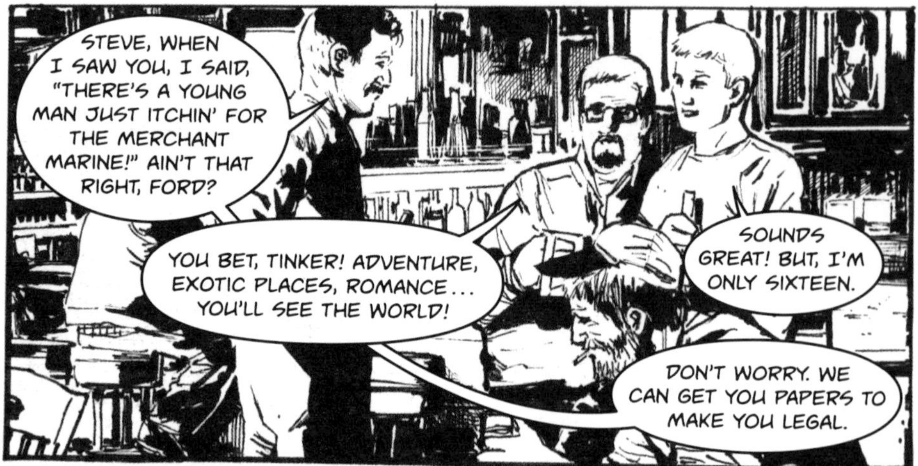
STEVE, WHEN I SAW YOU, I SAID, "THERE'S A YOUNG MAN JUST ITCHIN' FOR THE MERCHANT MARINE!" AIN'T THAT RIGHT, FORD?
YOU BET, TINKER! ADVENTURE, EXOTIC PLACES, ROMANCE... YOU'LL SEE THE WORLD!
SOUNDS GREAT! BUT, I'M ONLY SIXTEEN.
DON'T WORRY. WE CAN GET YOU PAPERS TO MAKE YOU LEGAL.

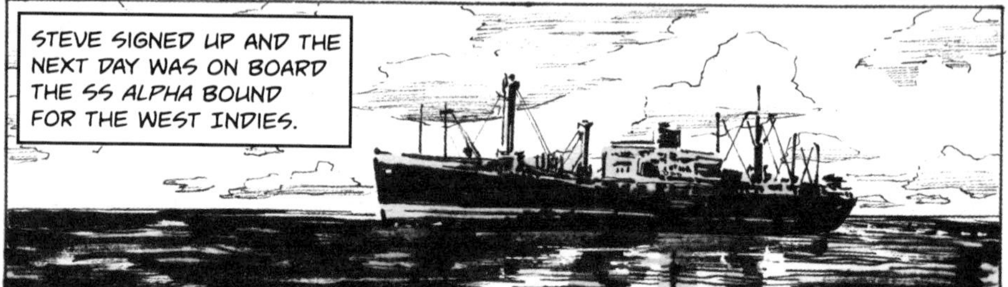
STEVE SIGNED UP AND THE NEXT DAY WAS ON BOARD THE SS *ALPHA* BOUND FOR THE WEST INDIES.

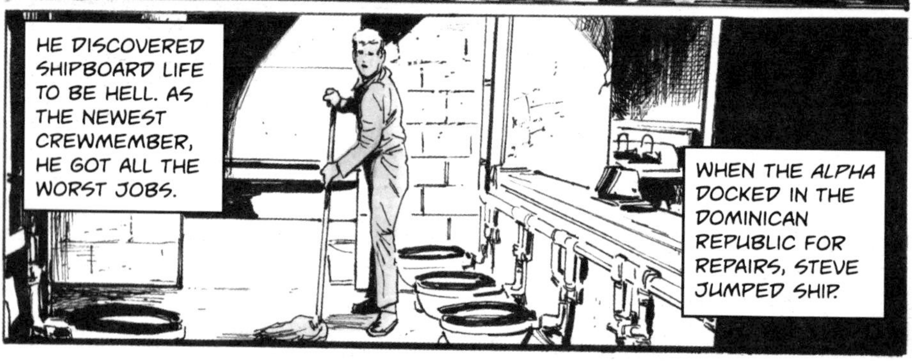
HE DISCOVERED SHIPBOARD LIFE TO BE HELL. AS THE NEWEST CREWMEMBER, HE GOT ALL THE WORST JOBS.
WHEN THE *ALPHA* DOCKED IN THE DOMINICAN REPUBLIC FOR REPAIRS, STEVE JUMPED SHIP.

FOR SEVERAL MONTHS STEVE LED A WIDELY TRAVELED ITINERANT LIFE--AS A TOWEL BOY AT A DOMINICAN BORDELLO, A ROUGHNECK IN TEXAS, A CARNIVAL VENDOR, AND A LUMBERJACK IN CANADA. THEN AT AGE 17, WHILE LIVING IN SOUTH CAROLINA, HE ENLISTED IN THE MARINE CORPS.

AFTER BOOT CAMP AND TRAINING, STEVE WAS STATIONED IN THE ARCTIC. DURING MANEUVERS THERE, HE RESCUED FIVE MARINES FROM A SINKING BOAT.

GIVE ME YOUR HAND!

IN RECOGNITION OF HIS HEROISM, McQUEEN WAS ASSIGNED TO PRESIDENT HARRY TRUMAN'S HONOR GUARD.

IN 1950, HE WAS HONORABLY DISCHARGED. HE RETURNED TO NEW YORK CITY TO SEE HIS MOTHER.

BUT, UPON ARRIVING AT HIS MOTHER'S APARTMENT BUILDING IN GREENWICH VILLAGE...

YOUR MOTHER LEFT SOME TIME AGO. MOVED TO SAN FRANCISCO.

STEVE DECIDED TO STAY IN THE VILLAGE AND JOINED THE BOHEMIAN LIFE OF THE THRIVING ACTING COMMUNITY.

ONE DAY, OVER COFFEE WITH AN ASPIRING ACTRESS FRIEND...

STEVE, WHY DON'T YOU COME DOWN TO THE NEIGHBORHOOD PLAYHOUSE WITH ME? THEY'RE HAVING AUDITIONS, AND YOU LOOK LIKE YOU MIGHT HAVE SOME TALENT STASHED AWAY IN YOU.

HE WATCHED A COUPLE OF SESSIONS. AFTER LEARNING THAT THE G.I. BILL WOULD PAY FOR CLASSES...

...STEVE ARRANGED AN INTERVIEW WITH DIRECTOR SANFORD MEISNER.

WHEN THE INTERVIEW CONCLUDED...

CONGRATULATIONS, STEVEN. YOU'RE IN.

THANK YOU, MR. MEISNER.

OUT OF 3,000 HOPEFULS, STEVE WAS 1 OF ONLY 72 STUDENTS HANDPICKED FOR THE SCHOOL'S METHOD-ACTING PROGRAM.

TWO

CRACKING THE THROTTLE

AFTER THE NEIGHBORHOOD PLAYHOUSE, McQUEEN WAS ACCEPTED IN THE HERBERT BERGHOF STUDIO. THIS WAS FOLLOWED BY SUMMER STOCK PERFORMANCES IN 1953 AND 1954. THEN, IN 1955, HE AUDITIONED BEFORE THE LEGENDARY LEE STRASBERG...

WHEN I PLAY MUSIC, NOTHING IS CLOSED TO ME.

McQUEEN'S PERFORMANCE OF A MONOLOGUE FROM *GOLDEN BOY*--A PLAY ABOUT A VIOLINIST WHO CHOOSES TO BECOME A BOXER--CONVINCED STRASBERG TO ACCEPT HIM.

McQUEEN HAD ALWAYS LOVED MOTORCYCLES. HIS FIRST BIKE WAS A 1946 INDIAN CHIEF. IN NEW YORK CITY, HE OWNED A HARLEY-DAVIDSON MODEL K THAT HE NOT ONLY USED FOR TRANSPORTATION...

...HE ALSO USED IT FOR RACING AT NEARBY LONG ISLAND CITY RACEWAY.

A CONSISTENT WINNER ON THE TRACK, AND THE PRIZE MONEY SUPPLEMENTED HIS IRREGULAR ACTING INCOME.

IT WAS DURING THIS TIME THAT McQUEEN LITERALLY CROSSED PATHS WITH A YOUNG ACTRESS AND DANCER, RUBY NEILAM SALVADOR ADAMS--BETTER KNOWN AS NEILE ADAMS.

HI. YOU'RE PRETTY.

SEE YA, NEILE!

AFTER SEVERAL PASSING ENCOUNTERS, STEVE FINALLY ASKED NEILE OUT. AT THE TIME SHE HAD THE LEAD ROLE OF BABE IN *THE PAJAMA GAME*. WHEN THE NIGHT'S PERFORMANCE AT BROADWAY'S SHUBERT THEATER WAS OVER, STEVE WAS WAITING...ON HIS HARLEY.

STAGE DOOR

HI, STEVE!

HI, NEILE. HOP ON--LET'S GO!

INSTEAD OF HAVING A ONE-NIGHT SEXUAL FLING, WHEN THEY GOT TO HIS APARTMENT THEY TALKED UNTIL SUNRISE AND DISCOVERED SHARED CHILDHOOD TRAUMAS.

NEILE DIDN'T KNOW HER FATHER. A CHILD IN THE PHILIPPINES DURING THE JAPANESE OCCUPATION IN WORLD WAR II, SHE HAD LIVED IN A PRISONER-OF-WAR CAMP.

POOR KID.

I GOT THIS SCAR FROM JAPANESE SHRAPNEL.

MY MOTHER'S AN ALCOHOLIC... MY STEPFATHERS BEAT ME...THERE WAS REFORM SCHOOL.

POOR KID.

THE RELATIONSHIP BLOSSOMED, AND STEVE SOON MOVED INTO HER MORE SPACIOUS APARTMENT ON WEST 55TH STREET.

FOLLOWING HER RUN IN *THE PAJAMA GAME*, NEILE LANDED A MAJOR ROLE IN THE MOVIE "THIS COULD BE THE NIGHT" AND WENT OFF TO HOLLYWOOD.

AS STEVE WAS BETWEEN JOBS, NEILE BOUGHT HIM A PLANE TICKET SO HE COULD BE WITH HER.

BUT, AT THE LAST MINUTE, HE DECIDED TO JOIN HIS MOTORCYCLE-RIDING FRIEND AND UPSTAIRS NEIGHBOR, JOURNALIST LIONEL OLAY, AND ANOTHER FRIEND ON A MOTORCYCLE TRIP TO CUBA. TO PAY FOR IT STEVE CASHED IN THE PLANE TICKET.

NEILE WAS NOT HAPPY.

THEY ARRIVED IN 1956 AT A TIME WHEN REVOLUTIONARY COMMUNIST GUERILLAS LED BY FIDEL CASTRO WERE GAINING THE UPPER HAND IN CUBA.

OLAY HAD INTERVIEWED CASTRO SEVERAL TIMES.

BUT THAT RELATIONSHIP DIDN'T MATTER. ACCOUNTS VARY ON WHAT EXACTLY HAPPENED, WHETHER THEY WERE ARRESTED AS SPIES FOR RIDING TOO CLOSE TO A FORT OR FOR TRYING TO SELL CONTRABAND...

...BUT THE RESULT WAS THAT STEVE AND THE OTHERS WERE THROWN INTO PRISON.

STEVE WIRED NEILE ASKING HER TO SEND BAIL MONEY. STILL ANGRY, SHE REFUSED.

WESTERN UNION

NEILE I LOVE YOU STOP IN JAIL STOP NEED BAIL...

INSTEAD OF LINING THEM UP BEFORE A FIRING SQUAD, CASTRO'S TROOPS CONFISCATED THEIR MOTORCYCLES AND RELEASED THE TRIO, WHO MANAGED TO RAISE CASH FOR AIRFARE BACK TO THE STATES.

NEILE GOT OVER HER ANGER, AND ON NOVEMBER 2, 1956, IN A SIMPLE CEREMONY PERFORMED BY A JUSTICE OF THE PEACE, STEVE AND NEILE WERE MARRIED.

I NOW PRONOUNCE YOU MAN AND WIFE.

THE YEAR 1957 PROVED PIVOTAL FOR STEVE'S CAREER. FIRST HE LANDED A MAJOR ROLE AS A DISTURBED YOUNG MAN ACCUSED OF MURDER IN "THE DEFENDER," A TWO-PART DRAMA CO-STARRING RALPH BELLAMY AND WILLIAM SHATNER FOR THE PRESTIGIOUS CBS TELEVISION SERIES *STUDIO ONE.*

I TOLD YOU HOW MANY TIMES, I HAD A HEADACHE-- I HAD A HEADACHE AND WAS SICK TO MY STOMACH!

HE WAS 27 YEARS OLD WHEN HE LANDED HIS FIRST MAJOR MOVIE ROLE--THAT OF TEENAGER STEVE ANDREWS IN THE B-MOVIE HORROR FILM *THE BLOB.*

DAVE! DOC HALLEN'S BEEN KILLED!

INDESCRIBABLE! INDESTRUCTIBLE! NOTHING CAN STOP IT!

THE BLOB

BUDGETED AT LESS THAN $300,000, IT WAS A HUGE HIT, GROSSING $12 MILLION IN ITS INITIAL RELEASE.

STEVEN McQUEEN ANETA CORP

17

OF THE TWO, IT WAS NEILE WHO HAD THE GREATER ACTING CAREER DURING THIS TIME--SHE WAS MAKING $50,000 A YEAR COMPARED TO STEVE'S $3,000. THEN, IN LATE 1957, THINGS CHANGED FOR McQUEEN.

THE POPULARITY OF TELEVISION HAD MUSHROOMED DURING THE 1950s. THE THREE NETWORKS OF NBC, CBS, AND ABC DOMINATED THE MARKET.

ONE OF THE MOST POPULAR TELEVISION GENRES WAS THE WESTERN.

CBS WANTED A SPIN-OFF OF *TRACKDOWN*, A SERIES ABOUT TEXAS RANGER HOLBY GILMAN (ROBERT CULP). THE PILOT FOR THE NEW BOUNTY-HUNTER SERIES WOULD AIR ON *TRACKDOWN*. IF RESPONSE WAS STRONG, THE SERIES WOULD GET THE GREEN LIGHT.

CULP, WHO KNEW McQUEEN FROM THEIR GREENWICH VILLAGE DAYS, RECOMMENDED HIM FOR THE ROLE OF BOUNTY HUNTER JOSH RANDALL.

"THE BOUNTY HUNTER" AIRED ON MARCH 7, 1958. AUDIENCE REACTION TO McQUEEN WAS SO GREAT THAT HE STARRED IN A SECOND *TRACKDOWN* EPISODE, "THE BROTHERS."

THE SHERIFF TELLS ME THAT RANGER'S STILL IN TOWN.

VIEWERS GOT A DOUBLE DOSE OF McQUEEN AS HE STARRED IN THE DUAL ROLES OF TWIN BROTHERS WES AND MAL CODY.

WHAT'S THE HARM IN THAT?

HE'S GOT NO BUSINESS HERE AT ALL. IF YOU CAN STEAL HIS GUN AND BADGE, THERE'S NO REASON FOR HIM TO BE HERE.

TO HELP HIS SHOW STAND OUT FROM THE OTHER WESTERNS, STEVE McQUEEN CARRIED A SAWED-OFF WINCHESTER. THE "MARE'S LEG," AS IT WAS CALLED, WAS JUST 19 INCHES LONG. AND BECAUSE IT WAS A REAL RIFLE, IT COST THE STUDIO $1,100 IN FIREARMS LICENSES.

WANTED: DEAD OR ALIVE DEBUTED IN THE PRIME-TIME SLOT OF 8:30 ON SATURDAY, SEPTEMBER 6, 1958. DURING ITS THREE-YEAR RUN, IT WAS A TOP 10 HIT. McQUEEN'S NEW FINANCIAL SECURITY GAVE HIM THE FREEDOM TO PURSUE HIS OTHER GREAT PASSION...

...RACING.

SOUTHERN CALIFORNIA WAS A MECCA FOR RACING AND STEVE, WANTING TO TAKE HIS DRIVING SKILLS TO THE NEXT LEVEL, BOUGHT A 1958 PORSCHE SPEEDSTER 1600 SUPER, A STARTER RACE CAR.

IN 1959, HE ENTERED NINE SPORTS CAR CLUB OF AMERICA RACES. HIS FIRST OFFICIAL RACE OCCURRED ON MAY 30, 1959, THE PRELIMINARY SANTA BARBARA COMPETITION. IT WAS ONE OF THE FEW TIMES HE QUESTIONED HIS DRIVING SKILLS.

STEVE, WHAT ARE YOU *DOING* OUT HERE?

BUT, WHEN IT WAS OVER, THE ROOKIE HAD FINISHED 11TH IN HIS CLASS--AND HE WAS HOOKED.

IN HIS SECOND RACE, THE NOVICE SANTA BARBARA HELD LATER THE SAME DAY, McQUEEN FINISHED FIRST IN HIS CLASS.

IN HIS NEXT THREE RACES, THE SANTA BARBARA, THE
PRELIMINARY HOURGLASS FIELD, AND THE HOURGLASS
FIELD, HE WAS DNS--DID NOT START.

ON JUNE 21, AT THE CONSOLATION HOURGLASS
FIELD DRIVING A PORSCHE 356 CARRERA,
McQUEEN AND CO-DRIVER EARL CALLICULT
FINISHED THIRD IN THEIR CLASS.

ON SEPTEMBER 5, AT THE PRELIMINARY
SANTA BARBARA, NOW DRIVING
A MORE POWERFUL LOTUS XI,
HE FINISHED SECOND
IN HIS CLASS.

THE NEXT DAY AT THE SANTA BARBARA, AND AGAIN DRIVING THE
LOTUS XI, HE WAS IN THE LEAD WHEN HE SPUN OUT, FINISHING 4TH.

ON SEPTEMBER 20, AT THE
SCCA REGIONAL DEL MAR,
AGAIN IN A LOTUS XI,
HE WAS IN THE LEAD
WHEN HE ACCIDENTALLY
HIT THE EMERGENCY
FUEL SWITCH ON
THE DASH, CUTTING
HIS POWER. HE
FINISHED 6TH
IN HIS CLASS.

AND WHEN HE WASN'T CAR
RACING ON THE TRACK...

...McQUEEN WAS OUT IN THE DESERT OFF-ROAD RIDING AND RACING. HIS FIRST OFF-ROAD BIKE WAS A 1959 TRIUMPH 500 PURCHASED FROM MOTORCYCLE SHOP OWNER, RACER, AND STUNTMAN BUD EKINS.

FOUR STAR STUDIO'S EXECUTIVES WERE HORRIFIED. THE LAST THING THEY WANTED WAS THEIR STAR INJURED OR KILLED IN A RACING ACCIDENT. UNDER PRESSURE FROM FOUR STAR, McQUEEN SOLD HIS LOTUS XI.

I'M COOL, MAN. I CAN AFFORD TO QUIT RACING FOR A WHILE.

NEEDLESS TO SAY, THAT "A WHILE" DIDN'T LAST LONG.

THREE

FULL THROTTLE ON THE SCREEN, ON THE TRACK, AND OFF-ROAD

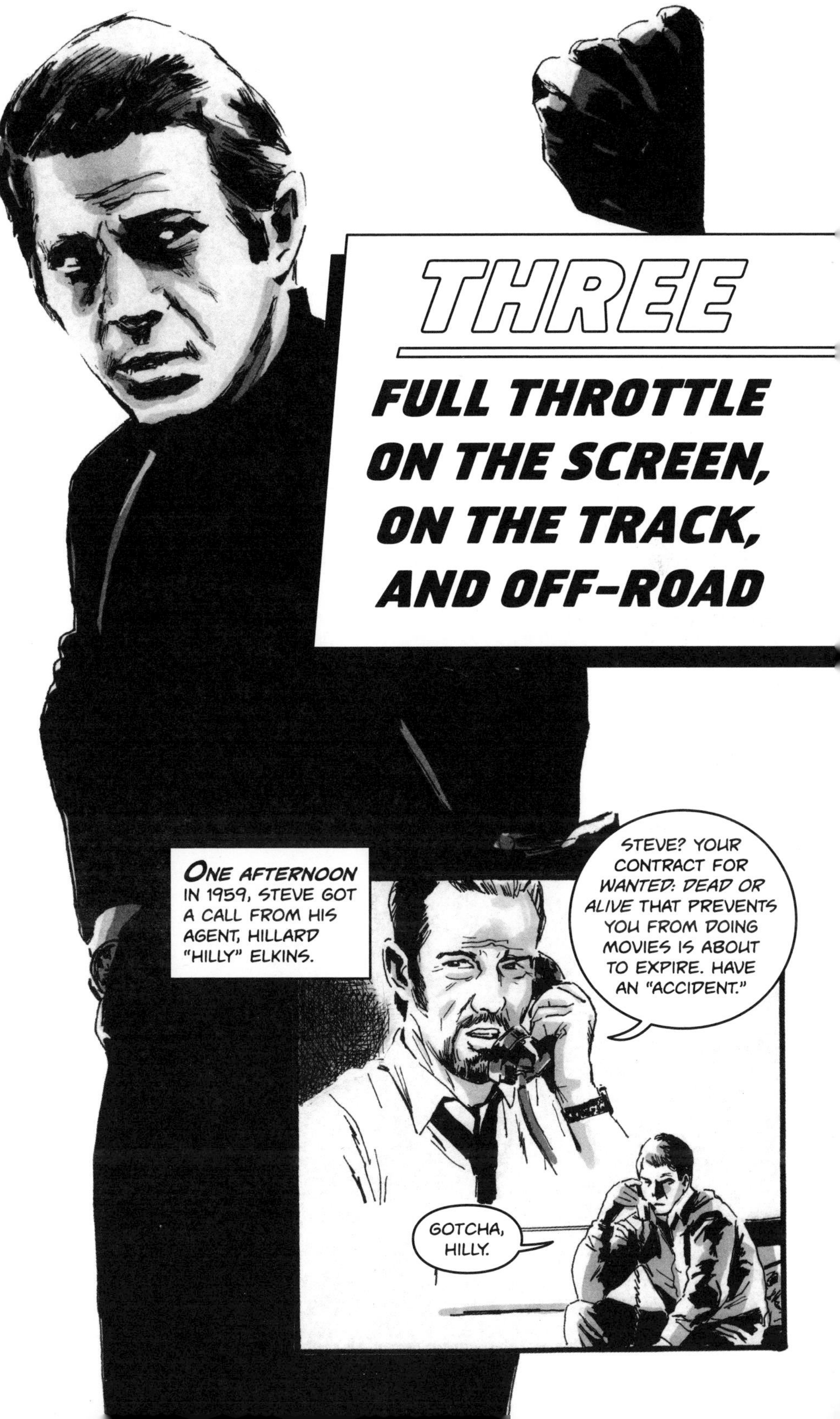

ONE AFTERNOON IN 1959, STEVE GOT A CALL FROM HIS AGENT, HILLARD "HILLY" ELKINS.
STEVE? YOUR CONTRACT FOR WANTED: DEAD OR ALIVE THAT PREVENTS YOU FROM DOING MOVIES IS ABOUT TO EXPIRE. HAVE AN "ACCIDENT."
GOTCHA, HILLY.

McQUEEN, ON A PROMOTIONAL TOUR FOR *WANTED: DEAD OR ALIVE* IN NEW ENGLAND, SUDDENLY LOST CONTROL OF HIS CADILLAC RENTAL CAR IN BOSTON. HE WALKED AWAY FROM HIS "ACCIDENT" WITH WHIPLASH.

K-RUNCH!

WITH AN INDUSTRY-WIDE STRIKE AFFECTING NEW PROJECTS IMMINENT, HILLY HAD THE NEGOTIATING TOOLS HE NEEDED TO REWRITE STEVE'S CONTRACT.

DICK, HERE'S THE DEAL: STEVE GETS TO DO MOVIES AND HIS SALARY IS DOUBLED.

WITH HIS THIRD-YEAR CONTRACT FOR *WANTED: DEAD OR ALIVE* SIGNED, STEVE WAS FREE TO ACCEPT THE MOVIE ROLE HE WANTED, THAT OF VIN TANNER IN *THE MAGNIFICENT SEVEN*.

BASED ON AKIRA KUROSAWA'S *THE SEVEN SAMURAI*, THE SEVEN GUNFIGHTERS BANDING TOGETHER TO HELP A MEXICAN VILLAGE FIGHT BANDITS WERE: YUL BRYNNER, STEVE McQUEEN, HORST BUCHHOLZ, CHARLES BRONSON, ROBERT VAUGHN, BRAD DEXTER, AND JAMES COBURN.

THE MOVIE OPENED ON OCTOBER 23, 1960, TO MIXED REVIEWS AND A DISAPPOINTING BOX OFFICE IN ITS INITIAL DOMESTIC RELEASE. BUT IN EUROPE, IT WAS A BIG HIT, AND IN A SECOND RELEASE IN AMERICA IT BECAME ONE OF THE HIGHEST-GROSSING FILMS OF THE YEAR.

THAT SAME YEAR, THE AMERICAN SPORTS CAR ASSOCIATION HONORED HIM WITH THE 1959 ROOKIE OF THE YEAR AWARD.

THANK YOU. THIS IS A GREAT HONOR.

BAD RATINGS, CAUSED BY A 1961 SCHEDULE CHANGE, LED TO *WANTED* BEING CANCELED. McQUEEN WAS NOW FREE TO PURSUE MOVIE PROJECTS. THE FIRST WAS *THE HONEYMOON MACHINE*, A DISASTER, FOLLOWED BY *HELL IS FOR HEROES*, WHICH BETTER DISPLAYED HIS METHOD-ACTING SKILLS.

IT WAS WITH HIS NEXT FILM, *THE WAR LOVER*, THAT McQUEEN HAD SOME REAL FUN--AWAY FROM THE SET.

SET IN 1943, *THE WAR LOVER* TOLD THE STORY OF B-17 PILOT CAPTAIN BUZZ RICKSON (McQUEEN), HIS LUST FOR WAR AND WOMEN, AND HIS TENSE RELATIONSHIP WITH CO-PILOT LIEUTENANT ED BOLLAND (ROBERT WAGNER). ULTIMATELY RICKSON DIES, CRASHING HIS DAMAGED B-17 INTO THE CLIFFS OF DOVER AFTER THE CREW HAS BAILED OUT.

START ENGINE NUMBER ONE.

ROGER.

BUT, WHAT EXCITED McQUEEN WAS THE FACT THAT IT WAS SHOT ON LOCATION IN ENGLAND. HE ARRIVED IN LONDON A MONTH AHEAD OF SCHEDULE SO HE COULD MEET RACING LEGEND STIRLING MOSS AND GET IN SOME RACING TIME.

STIRLING, IT'S AN HONOR TO MEET YOU.

A PLEASURE, STEVEN. COME, LET ME INTRODUCE YOU TO THE CHAPS AT BRANDS HATCH RACETRACK.

CAN'T WAIT.

BOB, MEET STEVEN McQUEEN, A SKILLED AMATEUR RACER AND SOMETHING OF AN ACTOR, SO I UNDERSTAND.

AS SOON AS I GET ON MY RACING GEAR.

HERE TO DO A SPOT OF RACING, MR. McQUEEN?

MOSS TOOK McQUEEN UNDER HIS WING AND GAVE HIM RACING POINTERS. THE TWO QUICKLY BECAME AS CLOSE AS BROTHERS.

COLUMBIA PICTURES, UNHAPPY ABOUT McQUEEN RACING, FORCED HIM TO SIGN AN AGREEMENT PAYING THE STUDIO $2.5 MILLION IF HE HAD AN ACCIDENT THAT DELAYED PRODUCTION. HE ALSO WASN'T SUPPOSED TO RACE DURING PRODUCTION...ORDERS HE IGNORED.

ONE DAY, NEAR THE END OF SHOOTING, STEVE WAS AT THE BRANDS HATCH RACING CIRCUIT IN A MINI COOPER. IT HAD RAINED, AND THE TRACK WAS SLICK.

SUDDENLY THE BRAKES LOCKED, CAUSING HIM TO DRIVE OFF THE TRACK.

FIGHTING TO CONTROL HIS CAR, HE NARROWLY MISSED OBSTRUCTIONS THAT WOULD HAVE WRECKED THE VEHICLE AND KILLED HIM.

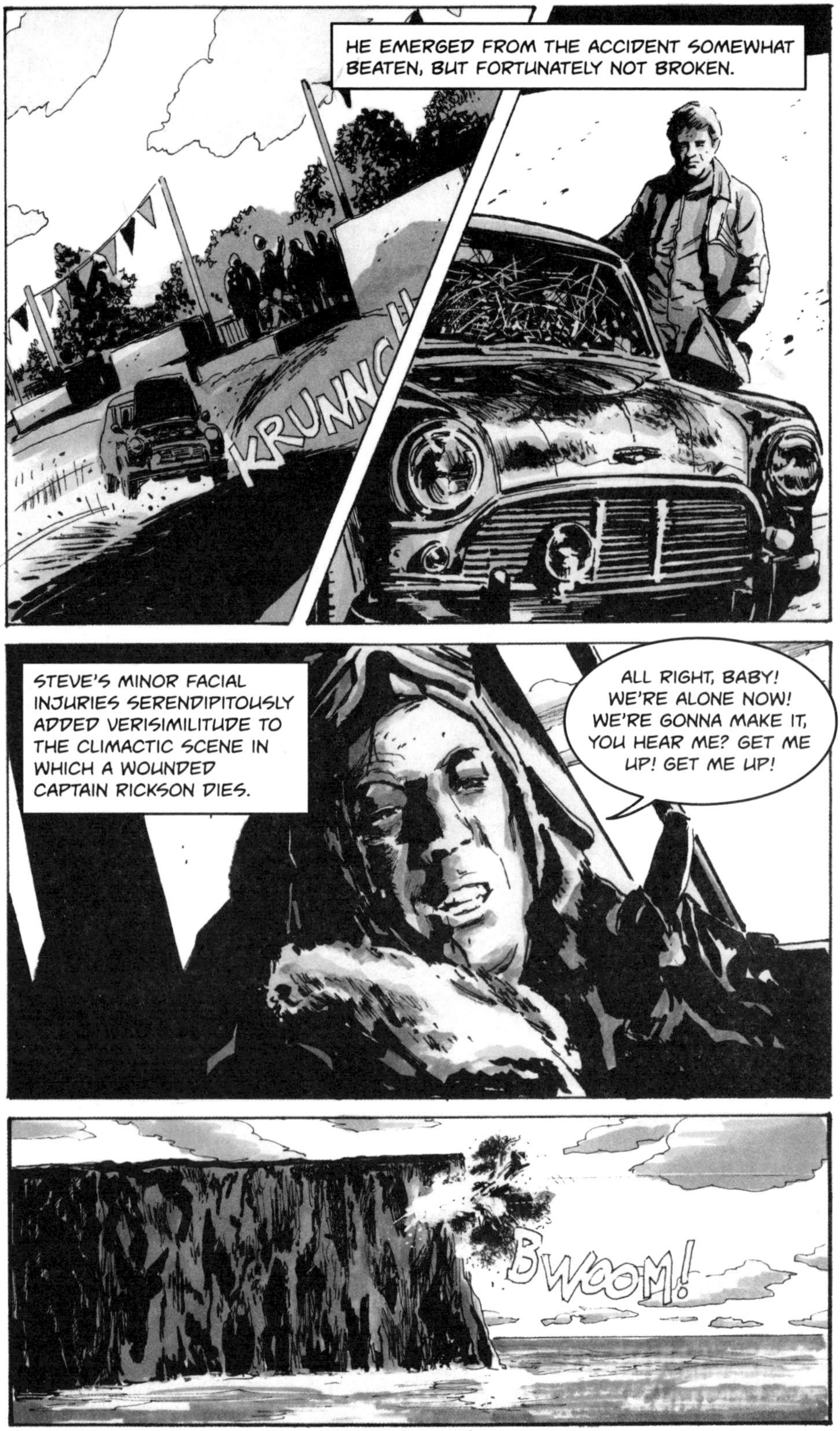
HE EMERGED FROM THE ACCIDENT SOMEWHAT BEATEN, BUT FORTUNATELY NOT BROKEN.
KRUNNCH
STEVE'S MINOR FACIAL INJURIES SERENDIPITOUSLY ADDED VERISIMILITUDE TO THE CLIMACTIC SCENE IN WHICH A WOUNDED CAPTAIN RICKSON DIES.
ALL RIGHT, BABY! WE'RE ALONE NOW! WE'RE GONNA MAKE IT, YOU HEAR ME? GET ME UP! GET ME UP!
BWOOM!

WITH FILMING COMPLETE, McQUEEN PREPARED TO RETURN TO CALIFORNIA AND RACING--THIS TIME AT THE WHEEL OF A COOPER T52 FJ HE HAD JUST PURCHASED.

I CAN'T WAIT TO GET THIS CAR ON THE SOUTHERN CALIFORNIA RACE TRACKS, STIRLING.

STEVE, THERE'S ANOTHER RACE I'D LIKE YOU TO CONSIDER--SEBRING. YOU'VE IMPRESSED THE CHAPS HERE AT BMC*...

...AND WE'D LIKE YOU TO BE A FACTORY TEAM DRIVER WITH US AT SEBRING IN MARCH.

A PROFESSIONAL RACE CAR DRIVER? YOU BET!

THOUGH STEVE KNEW ABOUT SEBRING, HE HAD NEVER DRIVEN ON IT. HIS DEBUT WOULD BE IN ITS FAMOUS ENDURANCE RACE, THE 12 HOURS OF SEBRING.

THE PRELIMINARY THREE-HOUR RACE WAS HELD ON SATURDAY, MARCH 23. WITH THE TRACK WET FROM RAIN, THE COURSE WAS DIFFICULT EVEN FOR EXPERIENCED DRIVERS. EVEN SO...

GOOD SHOW, McQUEEN! NINTH PLACE!

CASTROL

*BRITISH MOTOR CORPORATION

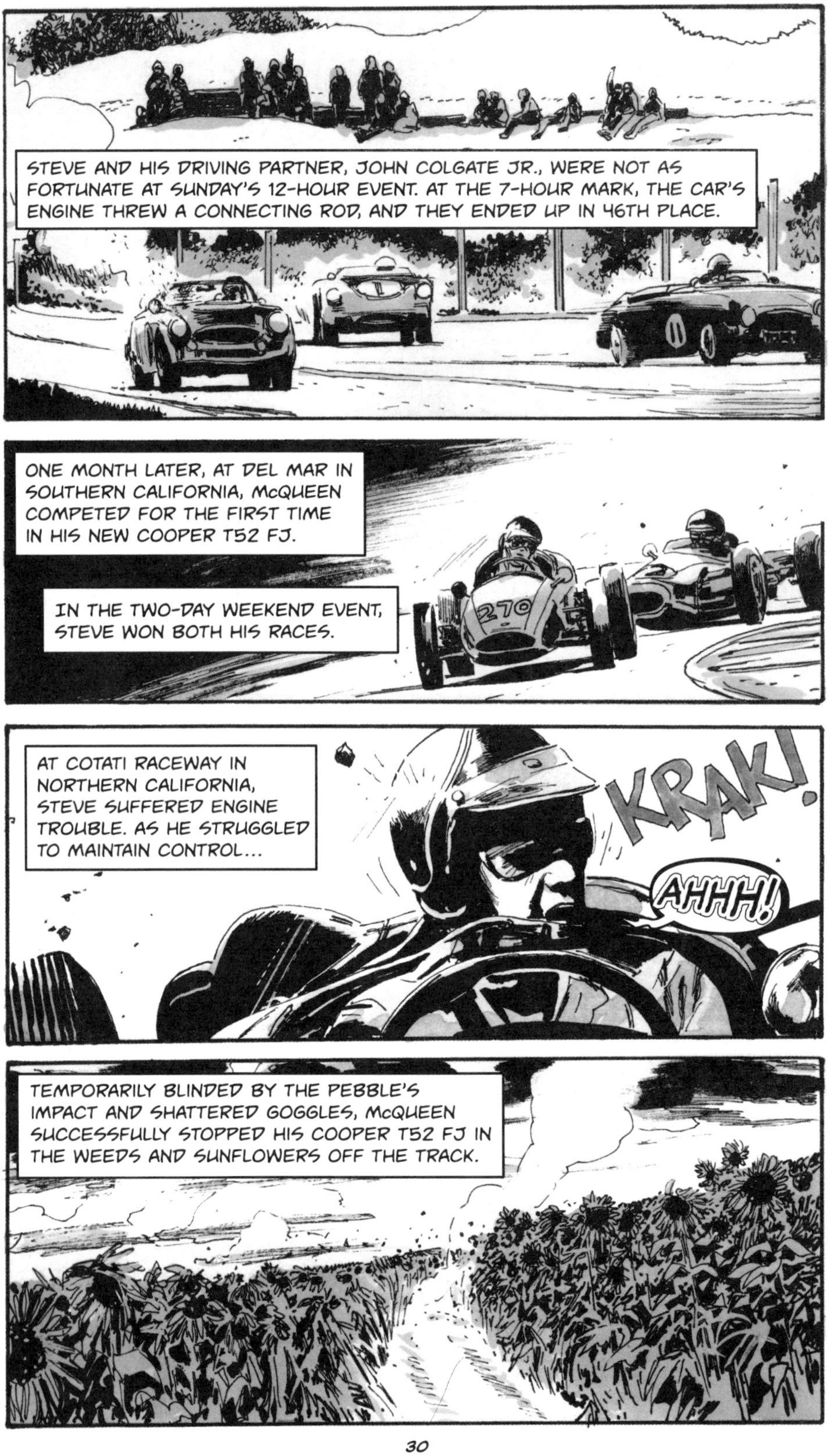
STEVE AND HIS DRIVING PARTNER, JOHN COLGATE JR., WERE NOT AS FORTUNATE AT SUNDAY'S 12-HOUR EVENT. AT THE 7-HOUR MARK, THE CAR'S ENGINE THREW A CONNECTING ROD, AND THEY ENDED UP IN 46TH PLACE.
ONE MONTH LATER, AT DEL MAR IN SOUTHERN CALIFORNIA, McQUEEN COMPETED FOR THE FIRST TIME IN HIS NEW COOPER T52 FJ.
IN THE TWO-DAY WEEKEND EVENT, STEVE WON BOTH HIS RACES.
270
AT COTATI RACEWAY IN NORTHERN CALIFORNIA, STEVE SUFFERED ENGINE TROUBLE. AS HE STRUGGLED TO MAINTAIN CONTROL...
KRAK!
AHHH!
TEMPORARILY BLINDED BY THE PEBBLE'S IMPACT AND SHATTERED GOGGLES, McQUEEN SUCCESSFULLY STOPPED HIS COOPER T52 FJ IN THE WEEDS AND SUNFLOWERS OFF THE TRACK.

IN ADDITION TO WINNING TWO MORE CAR RACES LATER AT SANTA BARBARA, HE WAS DIRT-BIKE RIDING IN THE DESERT WITH HIS FRIEND BUD EKINS.

MEANWHILE, HIS AGENT, HILLY ELKINS, WAS MAKING PLANS TO RETURN TO NEW YORK CITY. AS A PARTING GIFT, HE SENT STEVE THE SCRIPT OF A MOVIE TO BE DIRECTED BY JOHN STURGES.

McQUEEN HAD LIKED WORKING WITH STURGES ON *THE MAGNIFICENT SEVEN* AND THE 1959 FRANK SINATRA MOVIE *NEVER SO FEW*.

HE NEEDED A HIT NOW, OR HIS MOVIE CAREER, AT ITS MAKE-OR-BREAK POINT, WOULD BE OVER.

ELKINS THOUGHT THE STURGES PROJECT WAS SUCH A BREAKOUT MOVIE. IT ALSO OFFERED STEVE TOP BILLING FOR THE FIRST TIME.

HELLO, JOHN?

THE GREAT ESCAPE

YOU'VE GOT YOUR "COOLER KING."

THE GREAT ESCAPE

BASED ON PAUL BRICKHILL'S BOOK, *THE GREAT ESCAPE* IS THE STORY OF THE GREATEST ALLIED POW ESCAPE ATTEMPT DURING WORLD WAR II.

IN ADDITION TO McQUEEN, THE INTERNATIONAL CAST INCLUDED RICHARD ATTENBOROUGH, WHO PLAYED SQUADRON LEADER ROGER BARTLETT, THE ESCAPE'S MASTERMIND, AND GORDON JACKSON IN THE ROLE OF FLIGHT LIEUTENANT ANDREW MacDONALD, RESPONSIBLE FOR INTELLIGENCE.

HOW MANY YOU TAKING OUT?

TWO HUNDRED AND FIFTY.

TWO HUNDRED AND FIFTY?!?

McQUEEN'S CHARACTER, CAPTAIN VIRGIL HILTS, NICKNAMED THE "COOLER KING" BECAUSE OF HIS FREQUENCY IN THE ISOLATION CELL--THE "COOLER"--WAS BASED ON ARMY AIR FORCE PILOT DAVID JONES, WHO PARTICIPATED IN THE 1944 ESCAPE ATTEMPT FROM STALAG LUFT III.

THE CAST INCLUDED JAMES GARNER AND McQUEEN'S FRIEND JAMES COBURN. THOUGH STEVE HAD TOP BILLING, HIS CHARACTER, A SECONDARY ROLE VAGUELY DEFINED IN EARLY DRAFTS, WAS REDUCED IN LATER SCRIPT REVISIONS.

McQUEEN REBELLED AND REFUSED TO WORK UNTIL HIS ROLE WAS INCREASED. OUT OF THE SCRIPT CRISIS EMERGED THE MOVIE'S MOST FAMOUS SCENE.

STEVE, YOUR ROLE'S EXPANDED. YOUR BASEBALL-AND-MITT ROUTINE IS ALSO NOW A CONTINUOUS ELEMENT. WHAT ELSE CAN WE DO?

ADD SOMETHING AT THE END I'VE BEEN PUSHING FROM THE START!

THE MOTORCYCLE ESCAPE SCENE? OKAY, BUT FOR INSURANCE REASONS, SOMEBODY ELSE DOES THE JUMP.

OKAY. THEN THAT'S GOT TO BE MY STUNT DOUBLE, BUD EKINS.

TODAY, SUCH A STUNT WOULD BE DONE WITH COMPUTER ANIMATION. IN 1962, IT WAS SHOT LIVE. THE STUNT CALLED FOR EKINS TO MAKE A 60-FOOT LEAP WITH HIS MOTORCYCLE AND LAND BETWEEN TWO IMMENSE ROWS OF BARBED WIRE (ACTUALLY STRETCHED AND WRAPPED RUBBER).

MEASUREMENTS AND ESTIMATES WERE CAREFULLY MADE AND CALCULATED, A RAMP WAS CONSTRUCTED, AND EKINS REHEARSED. AS THE GERMAN BMW LACKED THE NECESSARY POWER FOR THE STUNT, EKINS RODE A MODIFIED BRITISH TRIUMPH 650, IMPERFECTLY CAMOUFLAGED TO RESEMBLE THE GERMAN MOTORCYCLE.

ON THE DAY OF THE SHOOT, EKINS GOT INTO POSITION, PULLED IN THE CLUTCH, GUNNED THE TRIUMPH'S ENGINE, DROPPED IT INTO GEAR WITH HIS RIGHT FOOT, RACED DOWN THE HILL GATHERING SPEED...SHOT UP THE RAMP...INTO THE AIR...

...OVER THE BARBED WIRE... AND LANDED IN THE OPEN SPACE BETWEEN THE TWO ROWS, PERFECTLY NAILING THE THRILLING STUNT ON THE FIRST TAKE.

AND, IN A BIT OF MOVIE TRIVIA, McQUEEN ALSO PORTRAYED ONE OF THE GERMAN MOTORCYCLIST PURSUERS IN THE SCENE--THUS, THROUGH MOVIE MAGIC, HE WOUND UP CHASING HIMSELF.

OF THE 76 P.O.W.S WHO ACTUALLY ESCAPED THE CAMP, ALL BUT THREE WERE CAPTURED. BUT ONLY 23 RETURNED ALIVE.

YOU WERE LUCKY, HILTS.

HOW MANY?

FIFTY.

THE GREAT ESCAPE WAS RELEASED ON JULY 4, 1963, AND DEDICATED TO THE FIFTY ESCAPEES WHO WERE RECAPTURED AND EXECUTED BY THE NAZIS. THE MOVIE WAS A CRITICAL AND BOX-OFFICE SUCCESS THAT QUICKLY BECAME A CLASSIC.

AS ELKINS HAD PREDICTED, IT VAULTED McQUEEN INTO STARDOM'S UPPER ECHELON.

COMPANY Presents

Steve McQUEEN · James GARNER · Richard ATTENBOROUGH

A GLORIOUS SAGA OF THE R.A.F.

COLOUR DE LUXE PANAVISION

JOHN STURGES

THE GREAT ESCAPE

STURGES · GLAVELL & BURNETT · BRICKE

BERNSTEIN A MIRISCH-ALPHA PICTURE

McQUEEN'S NEXT TWO MOVIES REFLECTED THE UP-AND-DOWN NATURE OF HOLLYWOOD. *SOLDIER IN THE RAIN* TANKED AT THE BOX OFFICE. *LOVE WITH THE PROPER STRANGER*, CO-STARRING NATALIE WOOD, WAS NOMINATED FOR FIVE ACADEMY AWARDS AND TWO GOLDEN GLOBES.

WHEN NOT IN FRONT OF THE CAMERA, HE WAS FAR AWAY FROM IT--COMPETING IN CROSS COUNTRY RACES LIKE THE 500-MILE, TWO-DAY GREENHORN ENDURO WITH BUD EKINS.

ON THE SECOND DAY OF THAT ENDURO, WHILE IN THE LEAD IN HIS CLASS AND 20 MILES FROM THE FINISH LINE...

DAMN! BLEW SOMETHING IN THE ENGINE!

BANG! KLAKAKLAK

McQUEEN LOST HIS FIRST-PLACE POSITION, BUT MANAGED TO FINISH THE RACE ON ONE CYLINDER.

THEN, ONE DAY...

STEVE, HOW ABOUT TAKING ON A REAL ENDURO CHALLENGE?

LIKE WHAT?

THE ISDT. I'VE COMPETED IN IT SOLO. NOW I'M PUTTING TOGETHER THE FIRST AMERICAN NATIONAL TEAM TO COMPETE--MY BROTHER DAVE, CLIFF COLEMAN, JOHN STEEN, AND...

...ME.

THE INTERNATIONAL SIX DAYS TRIAL (NOW CALLED THE INTERNATIONAL SIX DAYS ENDURO) IS THE "OLYMPICS OF MOTORCYCLING." FIRST RUN IN 1913, IT'S A COMBINATION STREET AND CROSS-COUNTRY TIMED RACE COVERING 1,200 MILES THAT IS THE ULTIMATE TEST OF MOTORCYCLE AND RIDER.

PARTICIPANTS COMPETE BOTH INDIVIDUALLY AND AS PART OF A NATIONAL TEAM AND ARE SCORED UNDER A POINT SYSTEM THAT INCLUDES BONUS POINTS FOR EARLY HEAT FINISHES AND PENALTY POINTS FOR LATE FINISHES. RACERS FROM 20 NATIONS ARRIVED TO COMPETE IN THE 1964 EVENT HELD ON SEPTEMBER 7–12 IN...

ERFURT, EAST GERMANY.

THIS WAS THE TIME OF THE COLD WAR, THE IDEOLOGICAL STRUGGLE BETWEEN WESTERN DEMOCRACIES AND EASTERN COMMUNIST STATES.

THE COMMUNISTS DIDN'T TRUST WESTERNERS--NOT EVEN TOURISTS.

WHAT IS THE PURPOSE OF YOUR VISIT?

WE'RE RACING IN THE ISDT.

AND YOU WILL USE THAT RACE AS AN EXCUSE TO SPY ON OUR COUNTRY, NICHT WAHR?

US? NO WAY. WE'LL HAVE OUR HANDS FULL JUST RUNNING THE COURSE!

THE AMERICAN TEAM'S DESERT RIDING EXPERIENCE WAS OF NO HELP IN THE FOREST, FIELD, AND MUDDY TRAILS TYPICAL IN EAST GERMANY. EAST GERMAN ROADS AND TRAILS HAD ANOTHER HAZARD NOT FOUND IN THE STATES...

...HORSESHOE NAILS.

THIS PRACTICE-RUN SOUVENIR IS A BIG SUCKER!

I'VE GOT THE EMERGENCY TIRE-REPAIR KITS: COMPRESSED AIR BOTTLE, TIRE IRON, AND TWO TUBES.

ABOUT 300 RACERS AND CREWMEMBERS PARTICIPATED IN THE 1964 EVENT. OPENING CEREMONIES INCLUDED A PARADE OF ALL THE NATIONAL TEAMS. McQUEEN HAD THE HONOR OF CARRYING THE AMERICAN FLAG.

RACERS WERE GIVEN NUMBERS BASED ON THEIR MOTORCYCLE'S ENGINE DISPLACEMENT. THE AMERICAN TEAM, WITH ITS LARGE ENGINES (ABOVE 350CC), HAD BIGGER NUMBERS. BUD'S WAS 250, JOHN'S WAS 266, CLIFF HAD 276, AND STEVE, RIDING A TRIUMPH TR6 650CC, HAD 278.

THE SMALLEST BIKES STARTED FIRST, AT 6 A.M. THEN AN HOUR AND A HALF LATER, STEVE, IN THE LAST GROUP, GOT THE GREEN FLAG TO GO.

IT RAINED THE FIRST DAY, MAKING THE COBBLESTONES SLIPPERY AND THE UNPAVED SECTIONS OF THE 264-MILE LEG MUDDY QUAGMIRES. EVEN SO, THEY ALL CLOCKED GOOD TIMES AT THE CHECKPOINTS.

DAMN, THOSE COBBLESTONES WERE SLICK! I DUMPED MY BIKE TWICE. JOHN?

I TOOK A SPILL, TOO, CLIFF. GOT SOME STITCHES. MY CHIN'LL HAVE A SOUVENIR SCAR.

AT THE END OF THE DAY, THOUGH TIRED, THEY WERE HAPPY WITH THE RESULTS: NO PENALTY POINTS AND IN GOOD STANDING ON BONUS POINTS.

ON THE SECOND DAY, WITH LIGHT RAIN FALLING JUST BEFORE THE RACE BEGAN, McQUEEN HAD TO MAKE AN EMERGENCY REPAIR.

TROUBLE, STEVE?

GAS TANK'S GOT A BROKEN SUPPORT BRACKET. THIS BUNGEE CORD SHOULD HOLD IT IN PLACE.

RESULTS ON THE SECOND DAY FOR THE TEAM WERE EVEN BETTER. THE POINT TOTAL AT DAY'S END PUT THEM IN GOOD SHAPE TO CHALLENGE FOR A GOLD MEDAL.

THOUGH DAY THREE STARTED WELL, WITH CLEAR WEATHER AND DRY CONDITIONS, THE TEAM'S FORTUNES TOOK A TURN FOR THE WORSE. FIRST, BUD SMASHED HIS TRIUMPH TR5 500 INTO A BRIDGE. THOUGH HE MANAGED TO FINISH, HIS RIGHT LEG WAS BROKEN, ENDING HIS RACE.

SKREEE-KPASI

THEN, STEVE AND CLIFF COLEMAN COLLIDED. THOUGH NEITHER WAS HURT, THE EXHAUST PIPE JOINT ON STEVE'S BIKE GOT PINCHED IN THE ACCIDENT, ROBBING THE ENGINE OF POWER.

K-BRAAM!

STEVE BEGAN PUSHING HIS BIKE DOWN THE TRAIL, FALLING FARTHER AND FARTHER BEHIND. AT ONE POINT HE SAW A WOODSMAN WITH AN AX AND...

KRAK!

...GRABBING THE AX, HE VENTED THE EXHAUST PIPE ABOVE THE PINCHED JOINT.

DESPERATE TO CATCH UP, HE RACED FULL THROTTLE DOWN THE REMAINING LEG OF THE ROUTE. UNFORTUNATELY, BY THIS TIME...

...OFFICIALS HAD RETURNED THE ROAD TO CIVILIAN USE.

OH, SH--

THE TWO RIDERS TOOK EVASIVE ACTION, NARROWLY MISSING EACH OTHER. UNFORTUNATELY...

K-RASH!!

...STEVE EMERGED WITH SOME MINOR CUTS AND BRUISES, BUT HIS BIKE WAS WRECKED. HIS RACE, AND THAT OF THE AMERICAN TEAM, WAS OVER.

RACING AS INDIVIDUALS DAVE, CLIFF, AND JOHN WERE STILL IN CONTENTION. WHEN IT WAS OVER...

DAVE, CLIFF-- CONGRATULATIONS ON YOUR GOLD MEDALS!

YOU KNOW, IF YOU HADN'T TAKEN THAT WRONG TURN AND GOT LOST THAT FIRST DAY, JOHN, YOU'D BE WEARING GOLD, NOT SILVER.

FOUR

BACK TO THE MOVIES

McQUEEN COMPLETED WORK ON TWO MORE MOVIES IN 1964, BOTH RELEASED IN 1965. THE FIRST WAS THE FORGETTABLE *BABY THE RAIN MUST FALL*, CO-STARRING LEE REMICK.

WHEREVER MY HEART LEADS ME... BABY I MUST GO.

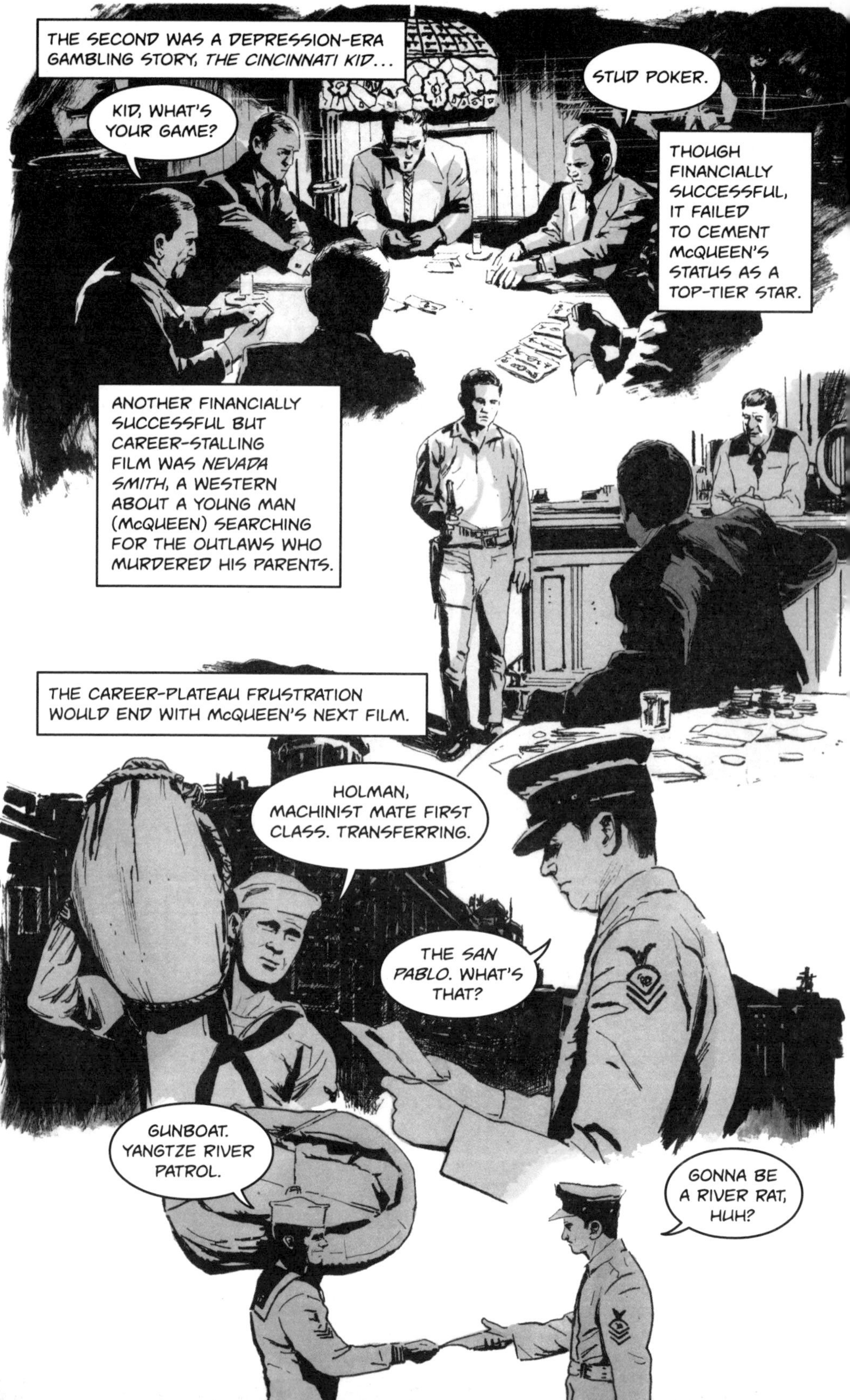
THE SECOND WAS A DEPRESSION-ERA GAMBLING STORY, *THE CINCINNATI KID*...
KID, WHAT'S YOUR GAME?
STUD POKER.
THOUGH FINANCIALLY SUCCESSFUL, IT FAILED TO CEMENT McQUEEN'S STATUS AS A TOP-TIER STAR.
ANOTHER FINANCIALLY SUCCESSFUL BUT CAREER-STALLING FILM WAS *NEVADA SMITH*, A WESTERN ABOUT A YOUNG MAN (McQUEEN) SEARCHING FOR THE OUTLAWS WHO MURDERED HIS PARENTS.
THE CAREER-PLATEAU FRUSTRATION WOULD END WITH McQUEEN'S NEXT FILM.
HOLMAN, MACHINIST MATE FIRST CLASS. TRANSFERRING.
THE *SAN PABLO*. WHAT'S THAT?
GUNBOAT. YANGTZE RIVER PATROL.
GONNA BE A RIVER RAT, HUH?

BASED ON THE RICHARD McKENNA NOVEL, *THE SAND PEBBLES* CO-STARRED RICHARD CRENNA, CANDICE BERGEN, AND McQUEEN'S CO-STAR FROM *THE GREAT ESCAPE*, RICHARD ATTENBOROUGH.

THE SAND PEBBLES

SET IN THE 1920s, IT'S THE STORY OF A FRACTIOUS CREW OF THE U.S. NAVY GUNBOAT *SAN PABLO* AND HOW THEY, AND A TEAM OF AMERICAN MISSIONARIES, FIGHT TO SURVIVE IN THE MIDDLE OF A VIOLENT CHINESE NATIONALIST UPRISING.

THE MOVIE PREMIERED ON DECEMBER 20, 1966, AND WAS A CRITICAL AND BOX-OFFICE SMASH. IT RECEIVED EIGHT ACADEMY AND GOLDEN GLOBE AWARD NOMINATIONS. McQUEEN RECEIVED HIS ONLY ACADEMY AWARD BEST ACTOR NOMINATION, LOSING TO PAUL SCOFIELD'S PERFORMANCE IN *A MAN FOR ALL SEASONS.*

the SAND PEBBLES

A ROBERT WISE PRODUCTION

STARRING STEVE McQUEEN

RICHARD ATTENBOROUGH · RICHARD CRENNA · CANDICE BERGEN

ALSO STARRING MARAYAT ANDRIANE · DIRECTED BY ROBERT WISE · SCREENPLAY BY ROBERT ANDERSON · BASED ON PRODUCTION DESIGNED BY BORIS LEVEN · MUSIC BY JERRY GOLDSMITH

AN ARGYLE·SOLAR PRODUCTIONS PICTURE · FILMED

MORE IMPORTANTLY, AS BIOGRAPHER MARC ELIOT HAS NOTED, BEFORE THAT MOVIE, "HOLLYWOOD HAD DEFINED WHAT A STEVE McQUEEN HERO SHOULD BE LIKE."

"AFTER *THE SAND PEBBLES,* *STEVE McQUEEN* DEFINED WHAT A HOLLYWOOD HERO WAS."

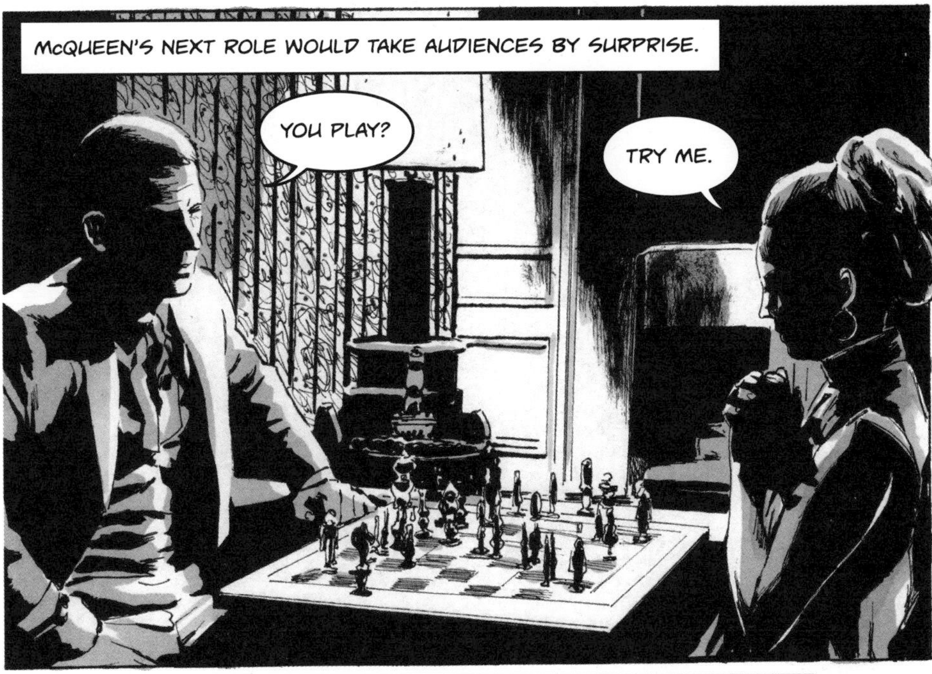
McQUEEN'S NEXT ROLE WOULD TAKE AUDIENCES BY SURPRISE.
YOU PLAY?
TRY ME.

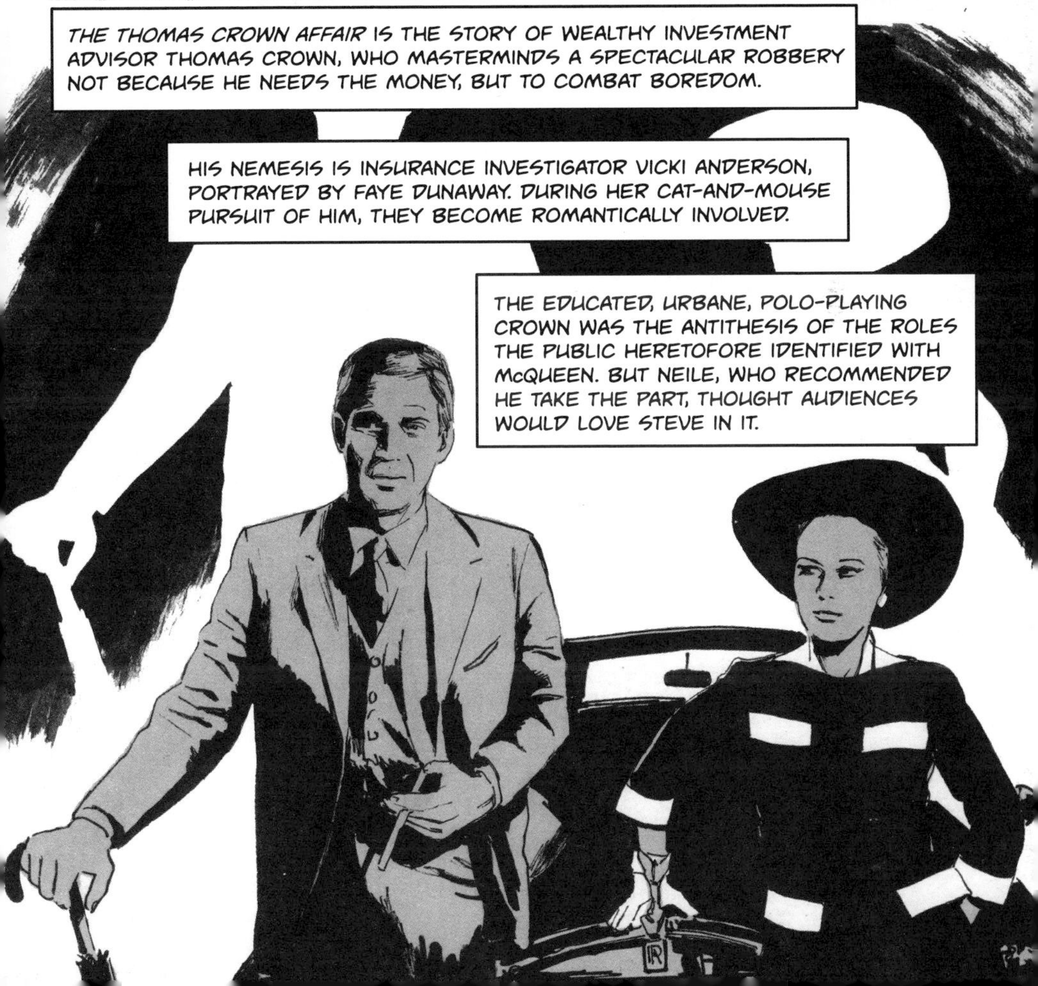
THE THOMAS CROWN AFFAIR IS THE STORY OF WEALTHY INVESTMENT ADVISOR THOMAS CROWN, WHO MASTERMINDS A SPECTACULAR ROBBERY NOT BECAUSE HE NEEDS THE MONEY, BUT TO COMBAT BOREDOM.
HIS NEMESIS IS INSURANCE INVESTIGATOR VICKI ANDERSON, PORTRAYED BY FAYE DUNAWAY. DURING HER CAT-AND-MOUSE PURSUIT OF HIM, THEY BECOME ROMANTICALLY INVOLVED.
THE EDUCATED, URBANE, POLO-PLAYING CROWN WAS THE ANTITHESIS OF THE ROLES THE PUBLIC HERETOFORE IDENTIFIED WITH McQUEEN. BUT NEILE, WHO RECOMMENDED HE TAKE THE PART, THOUGHT AUDIENCES WOULD LOVE STEVE IN IT.

AS WITH *THE GREAT ESCAPE*, McQUEEN PUT A MEMORABLE VEHICLE IMPRINT ON THE FILM--IN THIS CASE THE JOY-RIDING BEACH SCENES IN A MEYERS MANX DUNE BUGGY THAT McQUEEN HELPED MODIFY.

WE DID ONE BIG JUMP FOR THE CAMERA RIGHT OFF THE EDGE OF A HIGH DUNE, AND IT WAS WILD--WITH THE REAR WHEELS CLAPPIN' EACH OTHER IN THE AIR. I LOOKED OVER, AND FAYE WAS ALL BUG-EYED; THE BACK OF THE FLOORBOARD WAS SCRATCHED RAW FROM HER HEELS DIGGIN' IN.

THE THROTTLE JAMMED, AND WE WERE HEADING RIGHT FOR THE OCEAN AT A TERRIFIC RATE OF SPEED. WELL, ON FILM, ALL YOU COULD SEE WAS THIS ORANGE BUG DISAPPEARING INTO THE WATER. FAYE CAME OUT OF IT SOAKED AND SMILING. SOME TROOPER!

NEILE WAS RIGHT. AUDIENCES AND CRITICS LOVED STEVE IN THE MOVIE. IT WAS A SMASH HIT. HIS NEXT PROJECT WOULD PROVE EVEN BIGGER.

IMMEDIATELY AFTER SHOOTING *THOMAS CROWN*, McQUEEN BEGAN WORK ON *BULLITT*. STEVE WORKED CLOSELY WITH THE SAN FRANCISCO POLICE DEPARTMENT TO MAKE SURE HE GOT A PROPER FEEL FOR POLICE OPERATIONS IN THE CITY.

THE FILM, EXPENSIVE BECAUSE OF THE ACTION SEQUENCES AND EXTENSIVE LOCATION SHOOTING, WENT OVER BUDGET AND SCHEDULE.

BUT ULTIMATELY EVERYTHING PAID OFF--*BULLITT* WAS THE FIFTH HIGHEST GROSSING FILM OF 1968.

REVIEWS FOR *BULLITT* WERE GLOWING. *CHICAGO SUN-TIMES* MOVIE CRITIC ROGER EBERT BEST SUMMARIZED ITS SUCCESS: "STARS LIKE McQUEEN, BOGART, WAYNE OR NEWMAN AREN'T PRIMARILY ACTORS, BUT PRESENCES."

"THEY HAVE A MYTH, A PERSONAL LEGEND THEY'VE BUILT UP IN OUR MINDS DURING MANY MOVIES, AND WHEN THEY TRY TO PLAY AGAINST THAT IMAGE IT USUALLY LOOKS PHONY..."

"...McQUEEN IS GREAT IN *BULLITT,* AND THE MOVIE IS GREAT, BECAUSE DIRECTOR PETER YATES UNDERSTANDS THE McQUEEN IMAGE AND WORKS WITHIN IT. HE WINDS UP WITH ABOUT THE BEST ACTION MOVIE OF RECENT YEARS."

WITH *THE THOMAS CROWN AFFAIR* AT NUMBER 19, BY HAVING TWO MOVIES IN THE TOP 20, McQUEEN HAD SECURED HIS POSITION AS HOLLYWOOD'S BIGGEST SUPERSTAR, APTLY EARNING THE ACCOLADE "THE KING OF COOL."

FIVE

THE KING OF COOL

McQUEEN'S NEXT FILM ALSO WENT AGAINST TYPE. *THE REIVERS* WAS THE MOVIE ADAPTATION OF WILLIAM FAULKNER'S PULITZER PRIZE-WINNING NOVEL.

OLD MacDONALD HAD A FARM. E-I-E-I-OH!

STEVE LATER SAID THE MOVIE'S CAR, A CUSTOM REPLICA WINTON FLYER BUILT BY THE LEGENDARY VON DUTCH, WAS "THE REAL STAR OF THE PICTURE."

EVEN BEFORE HE BECAME AN ACTOR, McQUEEN WAS OBSESSED ABOUT PHYSICAL FITNESS. LATER, TO COPE WITH THE ENORMOUS PHYSICAL DEMANDS ON HIS BODY CAUSED BY RACING AND ACTING, McQUEEN BECAME A GYM RAT.

AS SOON AS HE COULD, HE INSTALLED A PRIVATE GYM AT HIS HOME...

...COMPLETE WITH A SWIMMING POOL. HIS REGULAR--WHEN POSSIBLE, DAILY--REGIMENS EMPHASIZED ENDURANCE AND THE MAINTENANCE OF A LITHE, SCULPTED LOOK OF HARD, BUT NOT OVERDEVELOPED, MUSCLES.

OBSESSION DEFINITELY WAS THE OPERATIVE WORD. McQUEEN HIRED CONDITIONING COACHES TO COME TO HIS HOME, THUS BECOMING A PIONEER IN THE USE OF PERSONAL TRAINERS.

MR. McQUEEN, THIS EXERCISE IS DESIGNED TO IMPROVE FLEXIBILITY. READY?

READY.

McQUEEN ALSO STUDIED MARTIAL ARTS. HE WAS ONE OF A NUMBER OF ACTORS WHO STUDIED JEET KUN DO, A HYBRID SYSTEM THAT EMPHASIZED MINIMAL MOVEMENTS TO ACHIEVE MAXIMUM EFFECT AND SPEED, CREATED BY BRUCE LEE.

AND McQUEEN WAS A PRIVATE STUDENT OF MARTIAL ARTS EXPERT CHUCK NORRIS.

McQUEEN LATER ENCOURAGED BOTH LEE AND NORRIS TO TAKE UP ACTING, WHICH BOTH DID TO GREAT SUCCESS.

53

FOR YEARS, STEVE HAD WANTED TO DO A RACING MOVIE. IN 1969, IT APPEARED STEVE'S DREAM PROJECT WOULD FINALLY BECOME A REALITY.

GREAT NEWS. THE STUDIO'S GIVEN ME THE GREEN LIGHT FOR *DAY OF THE CHAMPION* UNDER THE NEW NAME *LE MANS*. WE'RE GOING TO SHOOT IT DOCUMENTARY STYLE--FOCUSING ON THE CARS AND THE RACE. IT'LL BE THE WORLD'S MOST REALISTIC RACE CAR MOVIE.

THIS YEAR WE'LL ATTEND THE RACE, SCOUT OUT CAMERA LOCATIONS AND EVERYTHING. IN 1970 WE'LL RETURN AND FILM IT. THEN POST-RACE WE'LL SHOOT THE LOCATION SCENES WE NEED.

NOW, I WANT TO RUN THAT RACE. HERE'S THE CAR I PLAN TO USE-- A PORSCHE 908 SPYDER. IN THE RUN-UP TO LE MANS, I'VE PICKED THE RACES TO GET ME INTO SHAPE.

54

HIS FIRST RACE WAS IN FEBRUARY 1970 AT HOLTVILLE, A CONVERTED FORMER AIR FORCE FIELD IN SOUTHERN CALIFORNIA. IN THE MAIN EVENT HE LAPPED THE FIELD AND WON EASILY, SETTING A COURSE RECORD.

THIS WAS FOLLOWED BY A RACE AT RIVERSIDE. STEVE DID NOT FINISH, HIS CAR'S ENGINE SUFFERING A BROKEN GEARBOX.

ON MARCH 1, 1970, AT PHOENIX, McQUEEN AGAIN DOMINATED THE FIELD IN THE 17-LAP EVENT, WINNING THE RACE AND SETTING A NEW LAP RECORD.

NEXT UP WAS THE 12 HOURS OF SEBRING ON MARCH 21.

BUT, A FEW DAYS AFTER THE PHOENIX RACE...

HI, GUYS. HOW'S THE CAR?

SHE'LL BE READY FOR SEBRING...BUT... WILL YOU?

MR. McQUEEN--

--WHAT HAPPENED?

AFTER PHOENIX, McQUEEN HAD DECIDED TO TAKE HIS HUSQVARNA 400 AND, ENTERING UNDER HIS RACING ALIAS OF HARVEY MUSHMAN, RUN IN THE 3RD ANNUAL ELSINORE GRAND PRIX OFF-ROAD RALLY.

STEVE WAS IN THE TOP TEN WHEN HE TRIED TO JUMP OVER A DIP. INSTEAD...

...HIS HUSKY DOVE INTO IT.

AHHHHHH!

FORTUNATELY, NO BYSTANDERS WERE HURT. STEVE GOT BACK ON HIS BIKE--

--AND STILL FINISHED IN THE TOP TEN.

IT'S BROKEN. YOU'LL NEED AN X-RAY TO FIND OUT HOW BAD.

BUT, AN EXAMINATION OF HIS LEFT FOOT REVEALED ...

56

SO, STEVE, HOW BAD IS IT?

BROKEN IN SIX PLACES.

THAT COULD BE A PROBLEM--SEBRING MAY DISQUALIFY YOU FOR SAFETY REASONS. HOW ARE YOU GOING TO OPERATE A CLUTCH WITH A BROKEN LEFT FOOT?

WE'LL FIND OUT, WON'T WE?

THE TEAM FASHIONED A LEATHER BOOT TO FIT OVER HIS CAST, AND SEBRING OFFICIALS CLEARED HIM TO RACE.

THE NEWS WAS GREETED WITH SKEPTICISM BY THE OTHER RACERS.

YEAH, LOOKS LIKE A DAMNED HOTSHOT PUBLICITY STUNT.

WHAT THE HELL DOES THAT ACTOR THINK HE'S DOING? THIS IS AN ENDURANCE RACE!

MCQUEEN KNEW OF THE SKEPTICISM, LATER ACKNOWLEDGING THAT HE REGARDED SEBRING AS "THE MOST IMPORTANT RACE OF MY LIFE." HIS CO-DRIVER WAS PETER REVSON, HEIR TO THE REVLON FORTUNE AND AN ACCOMPLISHED RACE CAR DRIVER.

ODDS ARE AGAINST US WINNING, STEVE.

OUR 908'S 3-LITER POWER PLANT CAN'T KEEP PACE WITH THE 5.0 ENGINES IN THE PORCHE FACTORY-SPONSORED 917, THE ALFAS...

...AND THE FERRARI 12S. MARIO ANDRETTI'S LEADING THE FERRARI TEAM, AND HE'S THE ONE TO BEAT.

YOU KNOW WHAT THEY SAY IN RACING, PETE: "IN ORDER TO FINISH FIRST, YOU FIRST MUST FINISH." THAT'S WHAT WE'RE GOING TO DO.

AS REVSON PREDICTED, THEIR PORSCHE 908 WAS OVERSHADOWED BY THE MORE POWERFUL CARS. BUT AS THE RACE PROGRESSED, THE COMBINATION OF CONSISTENT DRIVING, ERROR-FREE PIT STOPS...

...AND OTHER CARS DROPPING OUT OF THE RACE SAW THE McQUEEN/REVSON ENTRY STEADILY ADVANCE.

THIS, DESPITE THE FACT THAT STEVE WAS RACING WITH A BROKEN FOOT.

PAIN IS...*BAD.* BUT, GOT TO DRIVE MY FULL TWO-HOUR SHIFT.

AT THE TENTH HOUR AND FINAL DRIVER HAND-OFF, THE McQUEEN/REVSON ENTRY WAS FIRST IN ITS CLASS AND IN *THIRD PLACE* OVERALL.

GO GET 'EM, PETE!

REVSON WAS IN THE LEAD GOING INTO THE FINAL 30 MINUTES OF THE RACE WHEN MARIO ANDRETTI, NOW DRIVING FERRARI TEAM CAR 21, CAUGHT—AND PASSED—REVSON.

McQUEEN AND REVSON FINISHED THE RACE IN SECOND PLACE OVERALL AND FIRST IN THE 3.0-LITER CLASS.

IN ADDITION TO THE SECOND-PLACE TROPHY, McQUEEN RECEIVED THE HAYDEN WILLIAMS MEMORIAL SPORTSMANSHIP AWARD FOR RACING WITH A BROKEN FOOT.

THE SUCCESS AT SEBRING SEEMED TO AUGUR WELL FOR THE MOVIE *LE MANS*.

THE *24 HOURS OF LE MANS* IS THE WORLD'S OLDEST AND MOST STORIED ENDURANCE RACE. AMERICAN WINNERS INCLUDE CARROLL SHELBY (1959) AND TEAMMATES A. J. FOYT AND DAN GURNEY (1967).

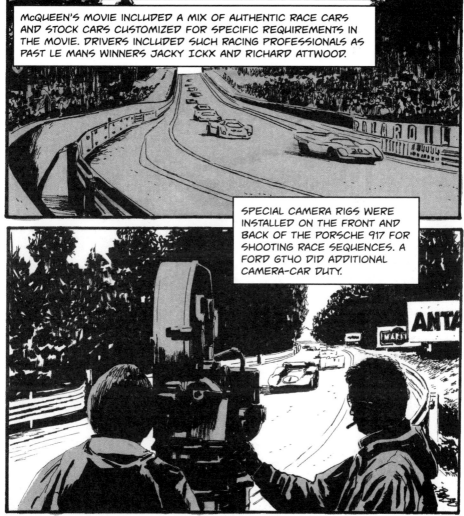

McQUEEN'S MOVIE INCLUDED A MIX OF AUTHENTIC RACE CARS AND STOCK CARS CUSTOMIZED FOR SPECIFIC REQUIREMENTS IN THE MOVIE. DRIVERS INCLUDED SUCH RACING PROFESSIONALS AS PAST LE MANS WINNERS JACKY ICKX AND RICHARD ATTWOOD.

SPECIAL CAMERA RIGS WERE INSTALLED ON THE FRONT AND BACK OF THE PORSCHE 917 FOR SHOOTING RACE SEQUENCES. A FORD GT40 DID ADDITIONAL CAMERA-CAR DUTY.

THE DRAMATIC BACK-TO-BACK FERRARI 512 AND PORSCHE 917 CRASH SEQUENCES ACTUALLY USED TWO STRIPPED-DOWN LOLAS WITH FERRARI...

K-RASSHH!

...AND PORSCHE BODIES.

CRUNNCH!!!

THE CARS IN THE CRASHES WERE REMOTE CONTROLLED BY A DRIVER IN A CHAIR DESIGNED BY THE SPECIAL EFFECTS TEAM.

BUT WHILE NOTHING WAS SPARED IN MAKING THE RACE REALISTIC, SIMILAR EFFORT WAS ALL BUT IGNORED REGARDING THE SCRIPT-- PRODUCTION ACTUALLY STARTED WITHOUT ONE.

THE SKELETAL PLOT IS ABOUT THE COMPETITION BETWEEN THE PORSCHE TEAM, LED BY MICHAEL DELANY (McQUEEN), AND RIVAL FERRARI TEAM, LED BY ERICH STAHLER (SIEGFRIED RAUCH).

ELGA ANDERSEN PLAYS LISA BELGETTI, WIDOW OF A DRIVER KILLED IN THE PREVIOUS YEAR'S RACE IN AN ACCIDENT INVOLVING DELANY.

THE MINIMAL DIALOGUE FUNCTIONS MORE AS BACKGROUND SOUND ON A PAR WITH THE ENGINE, PIT CREW, AND CROWD NOISE. THE FIRST MEANINGFUL DIALOGUE DOESN'T OCCUR UNTIL 40 MINUTES INTO THE MOVIE. McQUEEN'S ONLY MAJOR DIALOGUE OCCURS ONE HOUR AND 21 MINUTES INTO IT.

THIS ISN'T A THOUSAND-TO-ONE SHOT. IT'S A PROFESSIONAL BLOOD SPORT AND IT CAN HAPPEN TO YOU. AND THEN IT CAN HAPPEN TO YOU AGAIN.

WHEN PEOPLE RISK THEIR LIVES, SHOULDN'T IT BE FOR SOMETHING IMPORTANT?

WELL, IT'D BETTER BE.

BUT WHAT IS SO IMPORTANT ABOUT DRIVING FASTER THAN ANYONE ELSE?

A LOT OF PEOPLE GO THROUGH LIFE DOING THINGS BADLY. RACING'S IMPORTANT TO ME AS WELL. RACING...IS LIFE. ANYTHING THAT HAPPENS BEFORE OR AFTER IS JUST WAITING.

AS A MOVIE ABOUT RACING, LE MANS WAS EXCELLENT-- EVEN TODAY IT RECEIVES HIGH MARKS FROM RACING ENTHUSIASTS AND PROFESSIONALS. UNFORTUNATELY, ITS LACK OF STORY DOOMED THE FILM AT AMERICAN BOX OFFICES.

Steve McQueen takes you for a drive in the country. The country is France. The drive is at 200 MPH!

STEVE McQUEEN "LE MANS"

IRONICALLY, WITH *LE MANS* McQUEEN, A MOST AMERICAN OF ICONIC AMERICAN ACTORS, CREATED A FILM THAT IS VERY FRENCH-- NOT BECAUSE OF ITS SETTING, THOUGH THAT CERTAINLY HELPED.

Le MANS

WHILE IT WOULD BE A STRETCH TO COMPARE IT TO THE FRENCH NEW WAVE FILMS OF GODARD AND TRUFFAUT, THERE ARE ENOUGH NEW WAVE EXISTENTIALIST TROPES IN *LE MANS* TO SUGGEST IT IS A THOUGHT-PROVOKING HOMAGE.

UNFORTUNATELY FOR McQUEEN, AMERICAN AUDIENCES WERE EXPECTING ANOTHER *BULLITT*, NOT SOMETHING THAT WOULD MAKE THEM THINK.

CAN I GET YOU SOMETHING?

NO THANK YOU.

PREMIERED ON JUNE 23, 1971, AT INDIANAPOLIS, *LE MANS* WAS NOT ONLY A BOX-OFFICE FAILURE; IT BANKRUPTED McQUEEN'S PRODUCTION COMPANY, SOLAR, AND PUT THE FINISH TO HIS DETERIORATING MARRIAGE TO NEILE.

Divorce Decree

THOUGH SOLAR'S SEMI-DOCUMENTARY, *LE MANS*, WAS A BUST, ITS DOCUMENTARY *ON ANY SUNDAY*, RELEASED IN JULY, WAS A CRITICAL AND BOX-OFFICE SUCCESS, THOUGH NOT ENOUGH TO SAVE THE COMPANY.

BRUCE BROWN, WHO HAD DIRECTED THE SEMINAL SURFING MOVIE *THE ENDLESS SUMMER*, WANTED TO DO A SIMILAR PAEAN TO THE SPORT OF MOTORCYCLE RACING.

ON ANY SUNDAY

THE MOST EXCITING FILM EVER MADE ON MOTORCYCLE
BY BRUCE BROWN, PRODUCER OF THE ENDLESS S
RELEASED IN CANADA BY CRAWLEY FILMS

BROWN CONTACTED SOLAR FOR FINANCIAL BACKING, AND STEVE AGREED. HE HAD TWO REASONS FOR DOING SO. ONE WAS TO ADD CREDIBILITY TO HIS REPUTATION AS A SERIOUS BIKE RACER.

THE SECOND WAS HIS DISDAIN FOR HOLLYWOOD BIKER MOVIES IN GENERAL.

BRANDO'S MOVIE *THE WILD ONE* SET MOTORCYCLE RACING BACK ABOUT 200 YEARS.

MOST BIKE FLICKS IN THE PAST CONCENTRATED ON THE OUTLAW CRAP, HELLS ANGELS AND ALL OF THAT STUFF, WHICH IS ABOUT AS FAR AWAY FROM THE REAL WORLD OF MOTORCYCLE RACING AS I AM FROM LIONEL BARRYMORE.

THE DOCUMENTARY TELLS THE RACING STORIES OF THREE RIDERS--McQUEEN AND CHAMPION PROFESSIONAL RIDERS MERT LAWWILL AND MALCOLM SMITH.

THOUSANDS OF RIDERS COMPETE IN MOTOCROSS IN THE UNITED STATES. ONE OF THEM IS STEVE McQUEEN.

IF MOVIE STUDIO MOGULS REALIZED WHAT HE WAS DOING ON THAT SUNDAY AFTERNOON, THEY'D HAVE HAD HEART ATTACKS.

THE FINAL SCENE TOOK PLACE ON THE BEACH OF THE CAMP PENDLETON MARINE CORPS BASE. BROWN HAD TRIED TO GET PERMISSION BUT HAD BEEN STONEWALLED BY RED TAPE.

WHEN BROWN TOLD McQUEEN, STEVE MADE SOME CALLS. THE NEXT THING BROWN KNEW, HE HAD PERMISSION AND WAS ABLE TO FILM A STUNNING END FOR THE DOCUMENTARY.

ON ANY SUNDAY WAS NOMINATED FOR AN ACADEMY AWARD FOR BEST DOCUMENTARY. IT ACHIEVED McQUEEN'S GOAL OF CHANGING PUBLIC PERCEPTION OF MOTORCYCLE RACING AND EARNED AN AWARD FROM A GRATEFUL MOTORCYCLE INDUSTRY.

EVERY TIME I START THINKING THE WORLD IS ALL BAD, THEN I START SEEING PEOPLE OUT THERE HAVING A GOOD TIME ON MOTORCYCLES--IT MAKES ME TAKE ANOTHER LOOK.

MCQUEEN THEN STARRED IN TWO MOVIES DIRECTED BY SAM PECKINPAH WHO HAD DIRECTED THE HITS *THE WILD BUNCH* AND *STRAW DOGS*.

THE FIRST WAS *JUNIOR BONNER*, ABOUT AN AGING RODEO RIDER (McQUEEN) UNWILLING TO RETIRE AND HIS ATTEMPT TO RECONCILE WITH HIS ESTRANGED FAMILY.

THE FILM WAS ANOTHER BOX-OFFICE FAILURE.

THEIR SECOND COLLABORATION, HOWEVER, TURNED OUT BETTER.

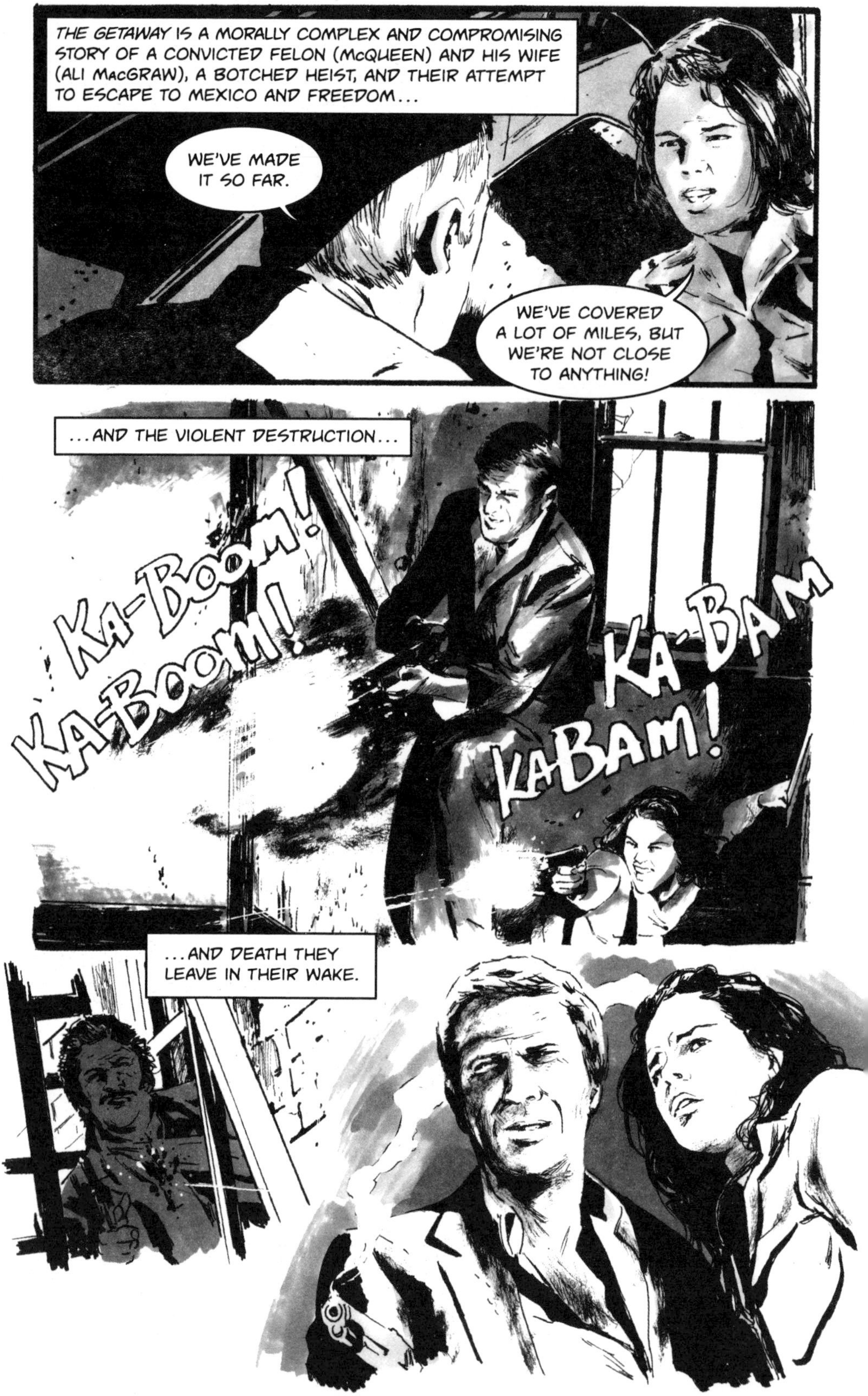
THE GETAWAY IS A MORALLY COMPLEX AND COMPROMISING STORY OF A CONVICTED FELON (McQUEEN) AND HIS WIFE (ALI MacGRAW), A BOTCHED HEIST, AND THEIR ATTEMPT TO ESCAPE TO MEXICO AND FREEDOM...
WE'VE MADE IT SO FAR.
WE'VE COVERED A LOT OF MILES, BUT WE'RE NOT CLOSE TO ANYTHING!
...AND THE VIOLENT DESTRUCTION...
KA-BOOM!
KA-BOOM!
KA-BAM
KABAM!
...AND DEATH THEY LEAVE IN THEIR WAKE.

THIS TIME, THE McQUEEN–PECKINPAH COLLABORATION WAS A BOX-OFFICE SUCCESS.

AGAINST COMPETITION THAT INCLUDED *THE GODFATHER*, *THE POSEIDON ADVENTURE*, *WHAT'S UP, DOC?*, *DELIVERANCE*, AND *JEREMIAH JOHNSON*, *THE GETAWAY* WAS THE 7TH HIGHEST GROSSING FILM OF 1972.

IT WAS ALSO A MOVIE IN WHICH STEVE McQUEEN AND ALI MacGRAW FELL IN LOVE. NOT LONG AFTER THE FILM'S RELEASE, MacGRAW DIVORCED HER HUSBAND. IN 1973, SHE MARRIED McQUEEN.

McQUEEN/MacGRAW

THE GETAWAY

McQUEEN'S NEXT MOVIE, *PAPILLON*, TOOK HIM TO HELL ON EARTH.

WE MAKE NO PRETENSE AT REHABILITATION HERE-- WE'RE PROCESSORS. A MEAT PACKER PROCESSES LIVE ANIMALS INTO EDIBLE ONES.

BASED ON THE BEST-SELLING AUTOBIOGRAPHY BY FRENCH CONVICT HENRI CHARRIÈRE, IT'S THE STORY OF A SAFE CRACKER UNJUSTLY CONVICTED OF MURDER, SENTENCED TO LIFE IN PRISON ON THE TROPICAL PENAL COLONY DEVIL'S ISLAND, AND OF HIS ONGOING ATTEMPTS TO ESCAPE.

WE PROCESS DANGEROUS MEN INTO HARMLESS ONES.

RELEASED IN DECEMBER 1973, *PAPILLON* WAS AN INTERNATIONAL BOX-OFFICE SMASH. IT WAS NOMINATED FOR AN ACADEMY AWARD, AND McQUEEN RECEIVED A GOLDEN GLOBE NOMINATION FOR BEST ACTOR IN A FILM.

McQUEEN PLAYED CHARRIÈRE. DUSTIN HOFFMAN PLAYED LOUIS DEGA, A FELLOW PRISONER THAT CHARRIÈRE BEFRIENDS.

THE NEXT YEAR, McQUEEN WOULD HAVE EVEN GREATER SUCCESS.

THE TOWERING INFERNO

DURING DEDICATION CEREMONIES OF THE WORLD'S TALLEST SKYSCRAPER, PUBLIC RELATIONS CHIEF DAN BIGELOW (ROBERT WAGNER) ORDERS ALL THE LIGHTS IN THE SKYSCRAPER TURNED ON. THIS OVERLOADS THE ELECTRICAL SYSTEM, CAUSING A FIRE IN A STORAGE ROOM ON THE 81ST FLOOR.

ARCHITECT DOUG ROBERTS (PAUL NEWMAN) CALLS TO WARN BUILDER JAMES DUNCAN (WILLIAM HOLDEN), WHO IS WITH CELEBRANTS IN THE PROMENADE ROOM ON THE 135TH FLOOR.

YOU'D BETTER THINK ABOUT GETTING THOSE PEOPLE UP THERE WITH YOU DOWN TO THE GROUND FLOOR.

WHAT FOR?

WHAT *FOR*?!? WE'VE GOT A *FIRE* HERE!

IF THAT FIRE WAS CAUSED BY FLUKY WIRING IN THIS BUILDING, WE COULD GET FIRES BREAKING OUT EVERYWHERE!

I AM NOT GOING TO CONCERN MYSELF WITH A FIRE IN A STORAGE ROOM ON 81, BECAUSE IT CAN'T POSSIBLY AFFECT US UP HERE.

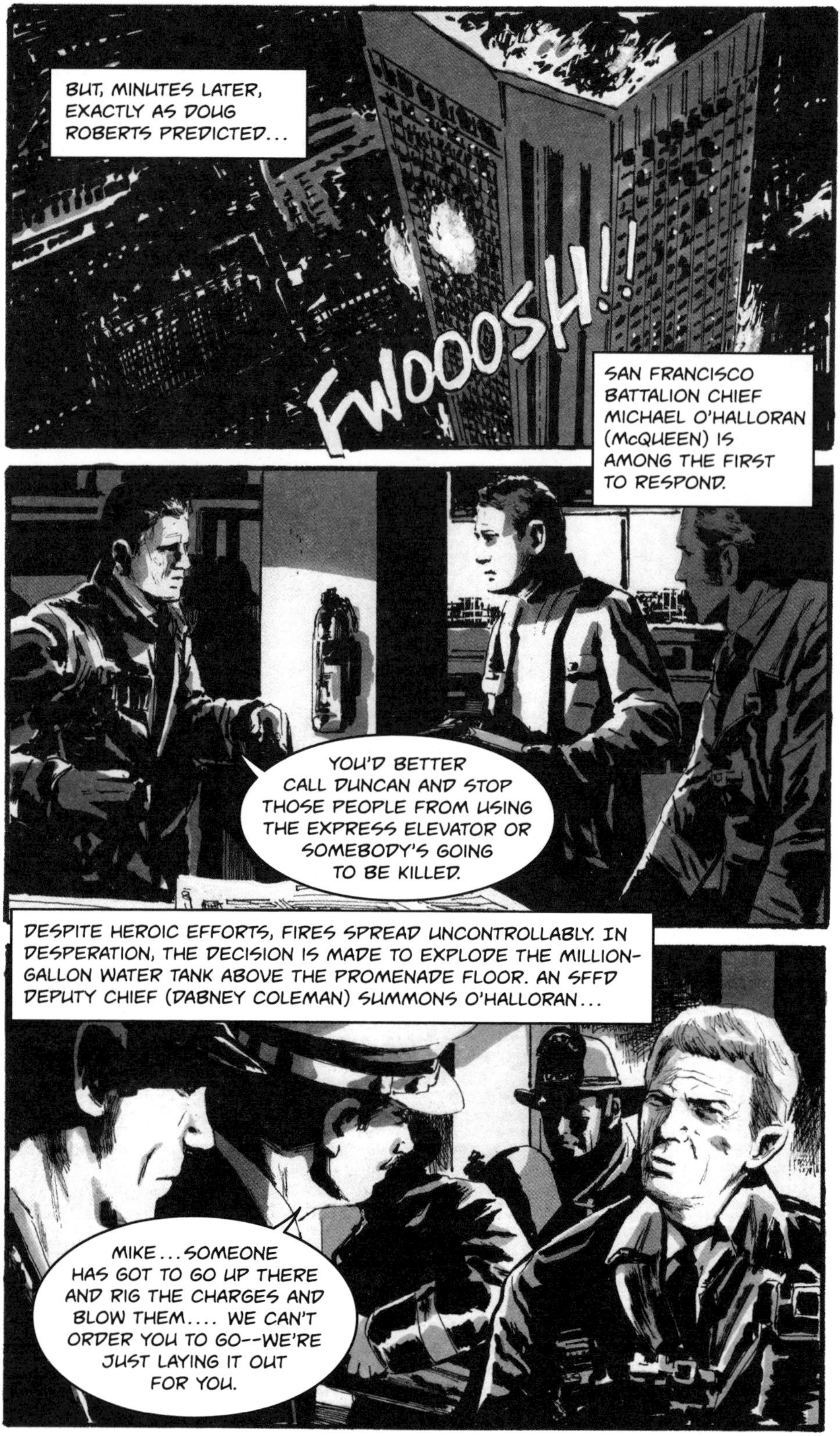

BUT, MINUTES LATER, EXACTLY AS DOUG ROBERTS PREDICTED...
FWOOOSH!!
SAN FRANCISCO BATTALION CHIEF MICHAEL O'HALLORAN (McQUEEN) IS AMONG THE FIRST TO RESPOND.
YOU'D BETTER CALL DUNCAN AND STOP THOSE PEOPLE FROM USING THE EXPRESS ELEVATOR OR SOMEBODY'S GOING TO BE KILLED.
DESPITE HEROIC EFFORTS, FIRES SPREAD UNCONTROLLABLY. IN DESPERATION, THE DECISION IS MADE TO EXPLODE THE MILLION-GALLON WATER TANK ABOVE THE PROMENADE FLOOR. AN SFFD DEPUTY CHIEF (DABNEY COLEMAN) SUMMONS O'HALLORAN...
MIKE...SOMEONE HAS GOT TO GO UP THERE AND RIG THE CHARGES AND BLOW THEM.... WE CAN'T ORDER YOU TO GO--WE'RE JUST LAYING IT OUT FOR YOU.

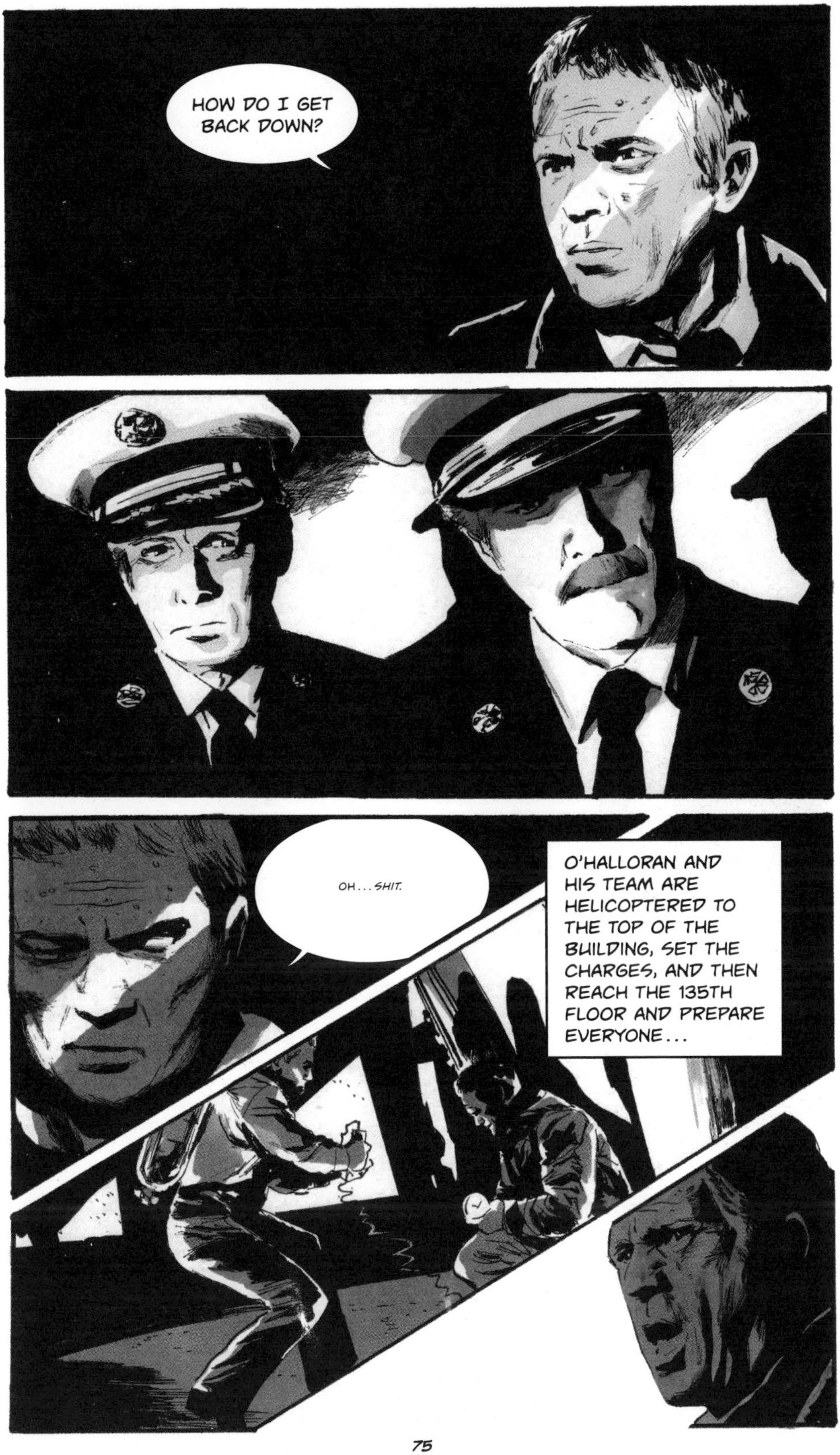
HOW DO I GET BACK DOWN?
OH... SHIT.
O'HALLORAN AND HIS TEAM ARE HELICOPTERED TO THE TOP OF THE BUILDING, SET THE CHARGES, AND THEN REACH THE 135TH FLOOR AND PREPARE EVERYONE...

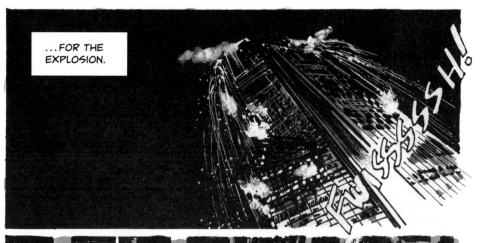

...FOR THE EXPLOSION.

RASSSH!

Y'KNOW, WE WERE LUCKY TONIGHT. THE BODY COUNT'S LESS THAN 200.

THE TOWERING INFERNO WAS A BOX-OFFICE BLOCKBUSTER, THE HIGHEST GROSSING FILM OF THE YEAR DURING ITS INITIAL RELEASE. NOMINATED FOR EIGHT ACADEMY AWARDS, IT WON THREE--BEST ORIGINAL SONG, CINEMATOGRAPHY, AND EDITING.

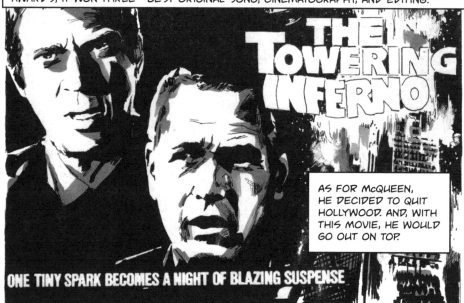

THE TOWERING INFERNO

AS FOR McQUEEN, HE DECIDED TO QUIT HOLLYWOOD. AND, WITH THIS MOVIE, HE WOULD GO OUT ON TOP.

ONE TINY SPARK BECOMES A NIGHT OF BLAZING SUSPENSE

SIX

SPEED SHIFTING

McQUEEN'S NEW LIFE PATH TOOK HIM PHYSICALLY AND PSYCHOLOGICALLY FAR FROM THE HECTIC HOLLYWOOD LIFESTYLE.

McQUEEN'S LIFE NOW REVOLVED AROUND HIS LIFELONG HABITS OF SMOKING MARIJUANA, DRINKING BEER...

...RIDING HIS DIRT BIKE...

...AND BEDDING BLONDES.

IN 1977, ALI MacGRAW, ANGRY OVER HIS SERIAL INFIDELITY AND CAREER-STIFLING CONTROL OF HER LIFE, FILED FOR DIVORCE, FINALIZED THE FOLLOWING YEAR. IN 1980, HE MARRIED BARBARA MINTY.

WHAT PEOPLE DIDN'T KNOW--AND WOULDN'T DISCOVER UNTIL AFTER HIS DEATH--WERE McQUEEN'S MANY HUMANITARIAN EFFORTS.

DURING THE SHOOTING OF *THE SAND PEBBLES*, STEVE AND NEILE MET FATHER EDWARD WOJNIAK, HEAD OF A GIRLS' ORPHANAGE. McQUEEN DONATED $12,500 ON THE SPOT AND FINANCIALLY SUPPORTED THE ORPHANAGE FOR YEARS.

AND EVERY YEAR AT CHRISTMAS, EASTER, AND THANKSGIVING, McQUEEN ARRIVED AT THE BOYS REPUBLIC TO GIVE THE STUDENTS GIFTS AND HOLIDAY MEALS.

HE ALSO DONATED MONEY TO THE REFORM SCHOOL AND WOULD REGULARLY SIT WITH THE STUDENTS AND TALK WITH THEM FOR HOURS.

ONE YEAR A LOS ANGELES RESTAURANT OWNER GAVE A FREE THANKSGIVING DINNER TO 50 AFRICAN AMERICAN ORPHANS. THE OWNER INVITED A NUMBER OF CELEBRITIES. STEVE WAS THE ONLY ONE TO APPEAR.

DURING LOCATION SHOOTING FOR *THE HUNTER*, McQUEEN, APPALLED BY THE POVERTY HE SAW IN THE CHICAGO GHETTO, ARRANGED TO HELP THE COMMUNITY THROUGH A CASH DONATION TO THE LOCAL CATHOLIC PARISH.

HE ALSO GAVE HIS STUNTMAN FRIEND LOREN JAMES MONEY TO BUY 100 BASEBALLS, FOOTBALLS, MITTS, AND BATS FOR NEIGHBORHOOD KIDS.

ONE DAY DURING THE SHOOTING OF A SCENE IN *THE HUNTER*, McQUEEN NOTICED A TEENAGE GIRL AMONG THE EXTRAS IN THE SCENE. WHEN HE ASKED WHY SHE WASN'T IN SCHOOL, SHE SAID, "BECAUSE I NEED THE MONEY." HER NAME WAS KAREN WILSON, AND McQUEEN DISCOVERED SHE WAS LIVING IN SQUALOR AND HER MOTHER WAS DYING. McQUEEN ASKED KAREN TO TAKE HIM TO HER MOTHER IN THE HOSPITAL.

IN THE LATE 1970s AFTER MOVING TO SANTA PAULA, CALIFORNIA, McQUEEN TOOK UP A NEW PASSION-- VINTAGE BIPLANE AIRCRAFT. INSTRUCTED BY RETIRED LOCKHEED TEST PILOT SAMMY MASON, McQUEEN GOT HIS PILOT'S LICENSE ON THE THIRD TRY.

CLOSE FRIENDS SUGGESTED THAT McQUEEN DID SO IN ORDER TO SPIRITUALLY CONNECT WITH HIS BIPLANE-FLYING FATHER.

WITH THE PEOPLE AT SANTA PAULA, McQUEEN WAS ABLE TO RELAX AND BE ANONYMOUS...

...SOMETHING HE CAME TO GREATLY VALUE.

SEVEN

LAST MOVIES AND FINAL DAYS

IN 1978, McQUEEN RETURNED TO ACTING, STARRING IN THE MOVIE *ENEMY OF THE PEOPLE*. THE MOVIE WAS SUCH A DISASTER IT WAS NEVER OFFICIALLY RELEASED.

IN 1979, McQUEEN AGREED TO STAR IN *TOM HORN*, A WESTERN ABOUT THE MAN WHO HELPED CAPTURE GERONIMO AND HAD THE MISFORTUNE OF OUTLIVING HIS LEGEND.

HIRED BY RANCHERS TO STOP CATTLE RUSTLERS, HORN'S BRUTAL METHODS BACKFIRE ON THE CATTLEMEN WHO CONSPIRE TO FRAME HORN FOR MURDER.

See him before he sees you.

PLAGUED BY PRODUCTION PROBLEMS, WHEN THE FILM WAS FINALLY RELEASED IN JULY 1980, IT PROVED OUT OF SYNC WITH THE TIMES AND WAS A BOX-OFFICE FAILURE.

the True Story

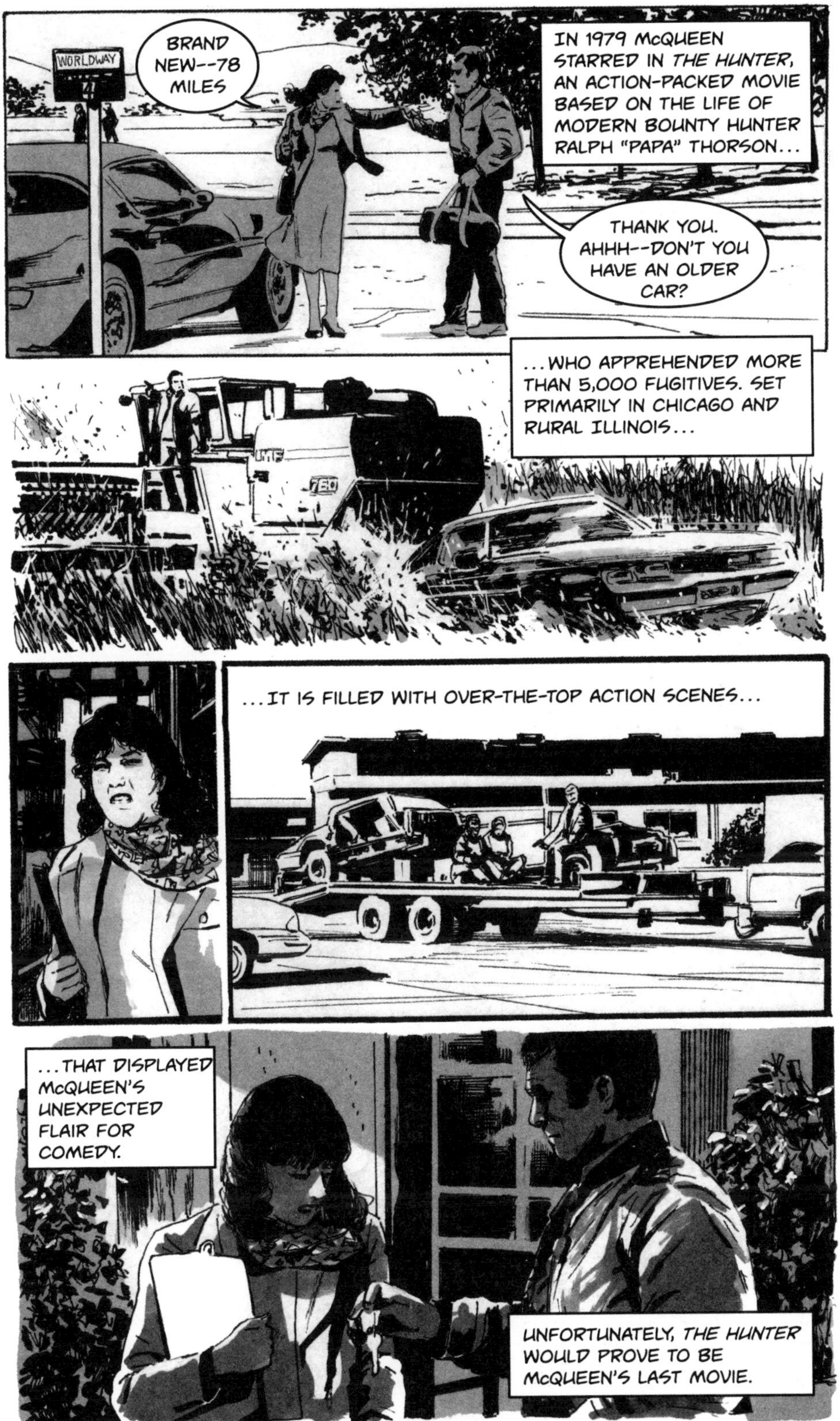
IN 1979 McQUEEN STARRED IN *THE HUNTER*, AN ACTION-PACKED MOVIE BASED ON THE LIFE OF MODERN BOUNTY HUNTER RALPH "PAPA" THORSON...
WORLDWAY
BRAND NEW--78 MILES
THANK YOU. AHHH--DON'T YOU HAVE AN OLDER CAR?
...WHO APPREHENDED MORE THAN 5,000 FUGITIVES. SET PRIMARILY IN CHICAGO AND RURAL ILLINOIS...
...IT IS FILLED WITH OVER-THE-TOP ACTION SCENES...
...THAT DISPLAYED McQUEEN'S UNEXPECTED FLAIR FOR COMEDY.
UNFORTUNATELY, *THE HUNTER* WOULD PROVE TO BE McQUEEN'S LAST MOVIE.

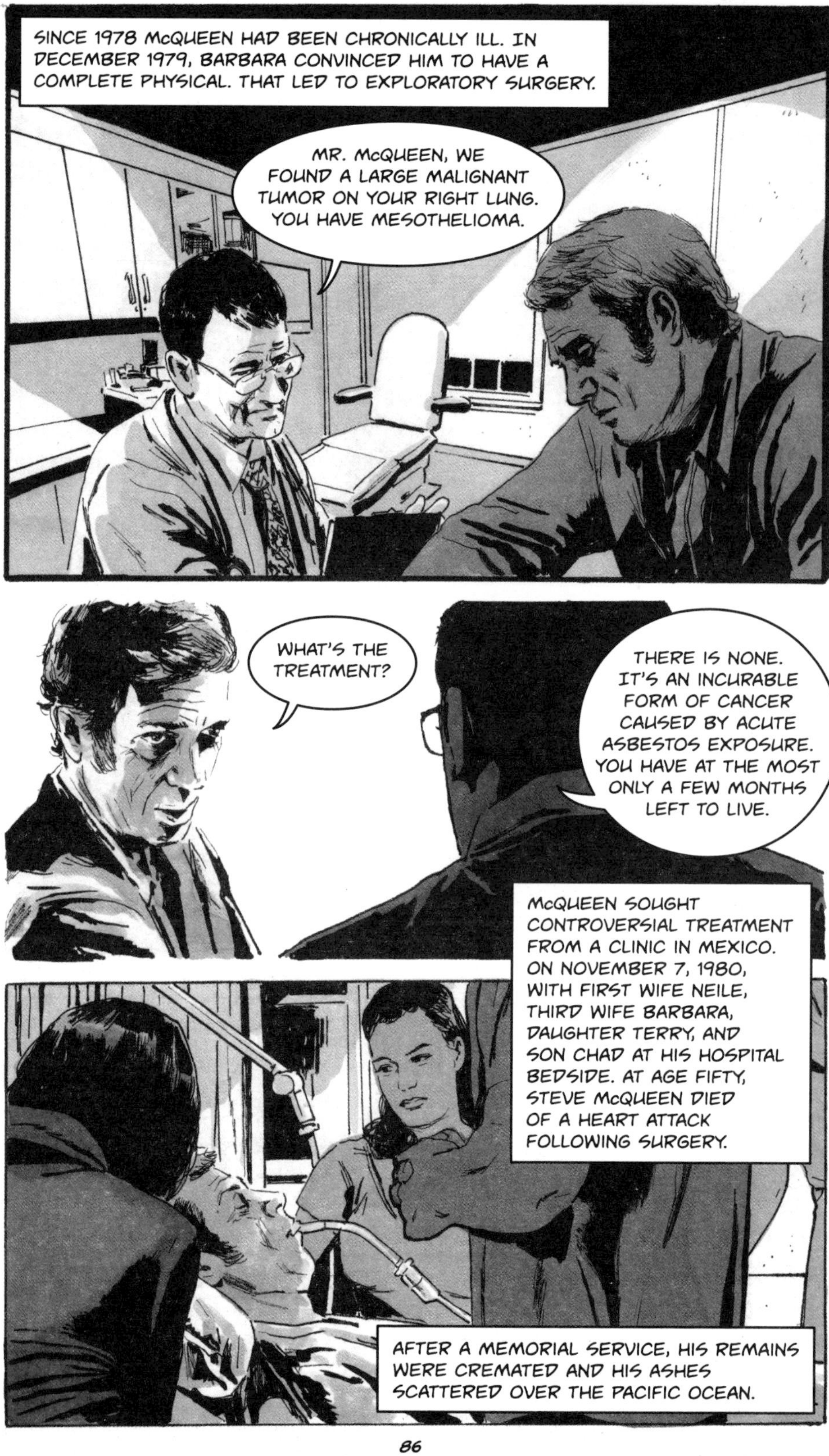
SINCE 1978 McQUEEN HAD BEEN CHRONICALLY ILL. IN DECEMBER 1979, BARBARA CONVINCED HIM TO HAVE A COMPLETE PHYSICAL. THAT LED TO EXPLORATORY SURGERY.
MR. McQUEEN, WE FOUND A LARGE MALIGNANT TUMOR ON YOUR RIGHT LUNG. YOU HAVE MESOTHELIOMA.
WHAT'S THE TREATMENT?
THERE IS NONE. IT'S AN INCURABLE FORM OF CANCER CAUSED BY ACUTE ASBESTOS EXPOSURE. YOU HAVE AT THE MOST ONLY A FEW MONTHS LEFT TO LIVE.
McQUEEN SOUGHT CONTROVERSIAL TREATMENT FROM A CLINIC IN MEXICO. ON NOVEMBER 7, 1980, WITH FIRST WIFE NEILE, THIRD WIFE BARBARA, DAUGHTER TERRY, AND SON CHAD AT HIS HOSPITAL BEDSIDE. AT AGE FIFTY, STEVE McQUEEN DIED OF A HEART ATTACK FOLLOWING SURGERY.
AFTER A MEMORIAL SERVICE, HIS REMAINS WERE CREMATED AND HIS ASHES SCATTERED OVER THE PACIFIC OCEAN.

NEWS OF HIS DEATH INSPIRED COUNTLESS TRIBUTES. *THE SAND PEBBLES* DIRECTOR ROBERT WISE SAID THE KEY TO McQUEEN'S POPULARITY WAS "THAT LEAN AND HUNGRY LOOK WHICH MEN IDENTIFY WITH AND WHICH AROUSES IN WOMEN THEIR MATERNAL INSTINCT AND THEIR DESIRE TO LOVE."

MOVIE CRITIC ROGER EBERT WROTE, "IN THE RIGHT ROLE, THERE WAS NO ONE ELSE QUITE LIKE HIM, AND FOR MR. McQUEEN THE RIGHT ROLE OFTEN MEANT A MAN OF ACTION INVOLVED IN EXCITING CHASES IN CARS, ON MOTORCYCLES, OR ON HORSEBACK."

AND, MORE THAN THIRTY YEARS AFTER HIS DEATH, HIS REPUTATION HAS NOT ONLY ENDURED BUT INCREASED. THE REASON, BIOGRAPHER MARC ELIOT EXPLAINED, WAS "STEVE McQUEEN IS ONE OF THOSE ACTORS WHO...BECAME A SEMINAL FORCE."

THE RACING WORLD ALSO PAID HOMAGE. MATT STONE, EXECUTIVE EDITOR OF *MOTOR TREND* AND *MOTOR TREND CLASSIC* MAGAZINES, WROTE THAT EVEN TODAY, "[McQUEEN] IS REVERED IN AUTOMOTIVE, MOTORCYCLING, AND MOTORSPORT CIRCLES."

WHETHER IN FRONT OF THE CAMERA OR ON A MOTORCYCLE OR IN A RACE CAR, THE KING OF COOL EARNED THE RESPECT OF HIS PEERS AND ADMIRATION OF HIS FANS BECAUSE HE LIVED HIS LIFE HIS WAY--*FULL THROTTLE.*